FLYING TIGER ARCHIVES

volume 1
1945-1965

Guy Van Herbruggen

designed by Simon De Rudder
edited by Charles Kennedy

Acknowledgements

When developing the Flying Tiger Memories book in 2019, I was constrained by the volume and sizing of the photos so came the idea to dedicate a book to photographic archives. I was able to create captions with context and detail thanks to the unique Flying Tigers Club archives newspaper clippings, and publications such as the Tigereviews and Tiger Rags.

Presented in chronological order and covering the first twenty years of the Flying Tiger Line (1946-1965), this book brings you the very best photos of the Flying Tigers Club archives (unless indicated, all the photos are from the FTC archives) as well as the finest slide scans and original photos from Jacques Guillem's collection, and from Peter Van Leeuw incredible CL-44 collection (see CL-44.com). Thank you both.

I am also indebted to Frank de Koster for helping me to photoshop some challenging slide scans, and Thomas Livesey who graciously shared Jon Proctor's Flying Tiger's photo collection. Thank you to "Mister DC-3", Michael S. Prophet, who shared Jan Boon's Connie slide scans.

I would like to record my appreciation to the following, for supplying photographic material, providing information or sharing some of their personal archives.

Everyone at the Flying Tigers Club who helped me and shared the same passion for the Flying Tiger Line, for encouragement, patience and contributions to this book, in particular John Burke, president of the FTC; Helena Burke, vice-president of the FTC; and John Dickson, Museum Director. None of this would have been possible without their help. John Dickson, in his dual role as FTLPA President, demonstrated encouragement and commitment to this book. Amongst the Flying Tiger Line Pilots Association staff, special thanks to George Gewehr, FTLPA Historian and Marshall Meyers, Attorney and son of Norman Meyers, FTL General Counsel and member of the Board of Directors. John, George and Marshall were always there, they never stopped me, they only encouraged me, and they always found answers to my questions. This is true Can-Do Spirit, thank you.

Thank you to Lydia Rossi, widow of AVG Captain Dick Rossi and Executive Secretary of the AVG Flying Tigers Association. Thank you also to Helena and John Burke for opening their home to me in Manhattan Beach during my multiple visits to LAX to dig in the archives of the Flying Tigers Club. Hvala!

I am once again forever indebted to my best friend, Charles Kennedy for his precious editorial help, keen insight, and ongoing support. That is solid friendship. It is because of his efforts, passion and commitment that we have a legacy to pass on to future generations.

Special thanks to Simon De Rudder, the ever-patient editor and his hard work in the design of this book.

Thanks to my publisher Astral Horizon Press — Bhavna Vadher, Steve Finnigan, Mathew Butler, and Sebastian Schmitz.

Last but not least, I have to thank my awesome wife, France for keeping the house and garden in order so I could work on the book. France was as important to this book getting done as I was. Thank you so much, my dear.

Thank you all for letting us serve the legacy of the Flying Tiger Line.

Guy Van Herbruggen
March 2023

FLYING TIGER ARCHIVES
Volume one, 1945 - 1965
Guy Van Herbruggen
ISBN 978-1-7396630-3-2
© 2023 Astral Horizon Aviation Press. All rights reserved.
www.theairlineboutique.com www.astralhorizon.co.uk

Preface

In 1945, the Flying Tiger Line was initially incorporated as the National Skyway Airfreight Corporation, employing the same unique and aggressive leadership style that served its founder, former AVG fighter pilot Robert W. Prescott, so well in combat under his presumed mentor, General Claire Chennault. Many colleagues from the American Volunteer Group, as well as other newly recruited employees, joined the new airline expecting something fun and different, but with no expectations of what the future would ultimately hold. Prescott's vision, transporting freight cheaply and efficiently by air, was a new concept which proved extremely successful as the years grew into decades. For many early employees, and most certainly all who followed during the next 44 years, an infatuation with a new idea became a sustained love affair – a Can Do Spirit which wrote the early and colourful history of the Flying Tiger Line.

If pictures are worth a thousand words, the images presented by author Guy Van Herbruggen and publisher Charles Kennedy speak volumes about the ingenuity, pride and dedication which contributed to the rich legacy of this remarkable company. An entirely new industry, airfreight, was created, and the Flying Tiger Line quickly emerged as the largest and most successful airfreight company in the world. The images in this book portray the esprit de corps in every team, the planning involved in every special flight, the excitement in every employee's life at being part of something big. The phrase, Anything, Anytime, Anywhere quickly became the corporate mantra. Flying Tiger employees made good on this promise with determination and ingenuity.

The wonderful pictures presented in this book may not have been possible were it not for the foresight of several employees dedicated to preserving the airline's legacy.

First and foremost are the efforts of Mister Joe Baker, hired in 1945 as employee #020. A central figure in FTL's success, he retired in 1978 as Director of Facilities and Equipment. During the mid 1980s, with rumours of impending acquisitions or hostile takeovers, Baker was proactive in accumulating and preserving historical material from all departments. Once the Flying Tiger/Federal Express merger was announced in 1988, he received cooperative support from chief executives at both Flying Tigers and Federal Express and was able to begin collecting and archiving company publications, public relations material and other important documents.

During this time, the Tiger Retirement Club was created, now known as the Flying Tigers Club. With Baker's coordination and direction, two offices were graciously provided by FedEx in the former Mosher Training Building at LAX. These eventually housed the enormous number of boxes, filing cabinets, shelves, models, and other memorabilia, which became the possession of the Club. Fred Reeves, a senior mechanic in the LAX Hangar, was named Museum Director and subsequently transformed the two storage rooms into an actual museum complete with display cases, model displays and filing cabinets full of FTL history. Tribute was paid to Baker by naming the new museum after him. On weekends and days off, Reeves would make himself available and open the museum doors to employees of the newly-merged company. Finally, gratitude must also go to the FedEx executives who understood the value of the precious archives in these rooms, still in the possession of the Flying Tigers Club to this day.

Because of many, most importantly the authors of this book, the proud Tiger Spirit displayed by Robert Prescott and his Flying Tigers will live on.

Captain John Dickson, FTL, FDX, ret.
Museum Director, Flying Tigers Club
President, Flying Tiger Line Pilots Association

Robert Prescott with his Curtiss P-40 in 1942 with distinctive tiger shark markings during his tour of duty under Claire Lee Chennault, commander and concept creator of the American Voluneer Group of pilots and mechanics to serve in China. The toothy decoration first appeared on the noses of the Curtiss P-40 Tomahawks of Royal Air Force No. 112 Squadron, fighting in North Africa. The intention was to inspire terror in adversary pilots. Initially known in late 1941 as the 'tiger sharks', the name evolved into Flying Tigers. The Walt Disney Studios voluntarily created the outfit's official symbol: a Bengal tiger, comically winged, flying through a victory "V". And so the Flying Tigers were born, and became famous for their unique and successful air combat manoeuvres.

Coming Home. Flying Tiger Robert W. Prescott, credited with downing six Japanese planes, returned home a hero to his mother G. W. Prescott and an awed young niece, Carolyn Prescott. He left Kunming, China, base headquarters of the 1st American Volunteer Group until the Flying Tigers were disbanded, on July 6, 1942, and flew 17,000 miles to get to Fort Worth, Texas. He and another AVG pilot from Texas, Paul Greene of Amarillo, hitched a ride on an army bomber and reached England by way of the Holy Land. They spent three days in England and Robert came home by way of Washington.

Destination Moscow. Washington National Airport May 7, 1943. President Roosevelt's emissary Joseph E. Davies, surrounded by crew members, shakes hands with Captain Waldon G. 'Swede' Golien and First Officer Robert Prescott on the right, between them smiling. The nine crew members of the Air Transport Command and a small group of civilians boarded a four-engined Douglas C-54-DO transport plane inside the hangar to preserve the utmost secrecy as to the identity of a statesman carrying a sealed briefcase. Their destination: Moscow. The C-54 used for this flight was Transcontinental & Western Air (TWA) ship #60, Army serial 42-32937. Passengers aboard the plane were Joseph E. Davies and his party, consisting of a physician, valet, naval aide and a Russian-speaking State Department official. Under the command of Captain Waldon G. Golien, former chief pilot for TWA requisitioned for the duration by the ATC, were First Officer Robert Prescott; navigators Peter H. Redpath and George H. Hart; radio operators Bill Davis and W. R. McGrew and Flight Purser Ernie A. Belshaw. Completing the crew were flight engineers Al E. Brick and Ted Vreeland. They knew little in advance about the flight until they read their orders. They had been instructed to make the trip as foolproof as possible and carried more than 370 spare parts in the cargo bins to ensure the ability to fly away after almost any technical failure imaginable. Davies was gone 27 days and traveled 25,779 miles, carrying a secret letter for Soviet leader Joseph Stalin. Because of the war raging in Europe, the aircraft could not fly over Europe, and so flew from New York to Brazil, to Dakar, Luxor, Baghdad, Teheran, Kuibyshev (today Samara), Stalingrad (today Volgograd), and on to Moscow. The party returned to the US via Novosibirsk and Alaska.

US Navy Budd RB-1 Conestoga fleet stored at Augusta, Georgia in 1945, before being flown to Long Beach, California
Jacques Guillem Collection

In 1945, former AVG pilot Robert Prescott negotiated with the War Assets Administration (WAA) for three former US Navy RB-1 Budd Conestogas, an all-stainless steel, rear-loading, twin-engine aircraft built by a company that had made its reputation manufacturing railways cars, on behalf of a new freight airline in Mexico called Aero-Azteca, following a November 1944 meeting in Acapulco with Samuel B. Mosher, a Los Angeles oil man representing the Signal Oil Company interested in having an airfreight line to run up and down the west coast of the United States and Mexico. Prescott delivered two Budds to Aero-Azteca that were soon confiscated by the Mexican government. The airline went out of business before ever carrying paying cargo. When it was learned that the entire production run of Budds would be sold, Prescott's brother suggested that the returned Flying Tigers buy the remaining aircraft themselves and start their own airline. Ten of the group pooled their resources, and for $10,000 each, Mosher's investors putting up half of the money and Prescott's Flying Tiger friends putting up their half. According to investor pilot Robert 'Catfish' Raine, "It was this inside knowledge that made the airline possible." On June 25, 1945, National Skyway Freight was founded by Robert Prescott and purchased the remaining 12 Budd Conestogas, immediately selling four of them to Asiatic Petroleum, allowing the recovery 58% of the entire purchase price.

A group of officials in front of the first Aero-Azteca Budd Conestoga BuNo 39307 (NC33308, msn # 016). Helen Ruth Prescott is second from the right.

Sold to National Skyways in July 1945, NC45347 is the third Budd RB-1 Conestoga built. The aircraft had a short career with the airline as it belly landed on the fairways of the Bluefield Country Club in Virginia in a blinding snowstorm at night on January 1, 1946. The plane was en route from New York to Los Angeles. There were seven people onboard: John McLaughlin, a passenger; O. E. Brown, flight engineer; John Pinney, co-pilot and former army flyer; Joe Rosbert, pilot and former Flying Tigers; Lieutenant J. P. Bosco, English naval officer, passenger; H. R. Miller, passenger and W. E. Green.

Robert Prescott (centre), president of the newly formed National Skyways Freight Corporation, with (left) Robert P. Hedman, vice-president operations and (right) Jack Cornelius, vice-president maintenance in a Chrysler automobile shown driven into cargo space of a Budd Conestoga, a sturdy transportation unit in the American land pioneer era.

First commercial flight. Flying Tigers ace Robert P. 'Duke' Hedman, vice president of flight operations, waves a bunch of carnations from the cockpit of a Budd Conestoga bound from Long Beach to the East Coast in August 1945. Ralph Meyers, a pioneering Bakersfield produce shipper, was National Skyway Freight's first customer. His two planeloads of fresh grapes destined for Georgia got the budding airline off the ground - literally.

Those grapes and strawberries look as if they were just picked. Well, that's pretty near the truth. The crates shown here are part of a shipment of 8,000 pounds of California-ripened fruit flown for wholesale grocers E. R. Godfrey & Sons. James Godfrey (left), treasurer, and J. D. Godfrey, president, inspect the fruit with Pilot Paul Kelly, who flew the plane from Salinas, California. This delivery marked the first all-freight transcontinental air service. Milwaukee Journal Picture

First air shipment of furniture. E.H. Warren, a Detroit mover, chartered a Flying Tiger Line Budd in August 1945 in the first shipment of household furniture by air for five Detroit families on their way to the West Coast. The photo was taken at the Detroit City Airport.

The first Budd Conestoga accident took place on Saturday August 25, 1945. NC45353 bellied into a field near Mount Olivet cemetery after losing its right engine on take-off from Detroit. The crew members were Captain John Robert Gordon, First Officer Dan Luskin and Flight Engineer Edward Garrett. They suffered minor cuts and bruises but the copilot picked up his suitcase and walked off into the night. He was never heard from again.

Eagles fly to keep gridiron appointment. On September 8, 1945, the Philadelphia Eagles, the first professional football club to move their squad by air, left Northeast Airport in two chartered 24-passenger Budd Conestogas of the National Skyways for Buffalo, where they met the Detroit Lions on Sunday, September 9th at the Buffalo Civic Stadium. 31 players, coaches, trainers, physicians, cameramen and members of the press brought the number of persons in the aerial safari to 40. After winning 35 to 7, the Eagles flew back to Philadelphia just after the Sunday's game.

News Reel Laboratory

Airshipped wine. On September 11, 1945, a Budd Conestoga aircraft flew a four-ton payload of muscatel, sherry and port of the Mission Bell Wine Company, from Fresno to New York La Guardia. The plane was piloted by Robert 'Duke' Hedman (centre in the picture, with sunglasses). This was the Flying Tigers' first cargo flight at La Guardia, where the picture was taken on arrival on September 12 and where several Flying Tigers were on hand and pitched in to help unload the 223 cases of wine.

Roundtrip charter. September 1945. Budd Conestoga NC45347 at the Buffalo Municipal Airport, N.Y. Unable to get seats on an airliner to the East to attend funeral services for international president of the Hotel and Restaurant Employes Edward Flore, 13 officials of the Santa Barbara Culinary Alliance employees chartered a National Skyways Budd for a roundtrip from Long Beach to Buffalo. The plane, piloted by Camille Joseph Rosbert (centre) and Richard Swyer, was without passenger comforts. The noise from the engines precluded talking and the passengers wrote notes to each other during the flight.

Sharing the ride. Enlisted men, 118 of them, off the United States Navy cruiser USS Astoria, just back from the Pacific, chartered five Budds of National Skyways at Long Beach Airport for a faster trip home. Most of the men were heading for the east coast, on 25-day leaves, although stops were made. On November 2, 1945, the planes left New York back to Long Beach, picking up men en route. The picture shows the Navy sailors boarding one of the transports on their way back to their ship.

First express plane into Memphis. October 1945. Budd Conestoga NC45347 winged its way from Detroit to Memphis, Tennessee. It was the first chartered, all-express plane to bring air freight to Memphis. The consignment consisted of the first postwar shipment of vacuum cleaners and cordless electric irons, flown to Woodson and Bozeman, Inc., from Detroit. The crew consisted of Captain Robert P. Hedman, vice president of the Flying Tiger Line, First Officer Josiah Bacon, who was a Navy carrier pilot, and Flight Engineer Robert Worth, formerly in the Flying Tigers. Hitchings Commercial Photographers

Flying horses. American turf horses were airlifted for the first time on October 22, 1945 from Los Angeles Municipal Airport to Bay Meadows in San Mateo, California. From left to right are Major William Hoelle, former Army ace; Stuart Hamblen, cowboy; and Robert Prescott, between the two thoroughbreds El Lobo and Featherfoot, in the Budd equipped with specially built stalls. The trip of about 380 miles was made in two hours and 50 minutes flown by Hoelle and Prescott. After an uneventful trip, they landed between the Bay Meadows horseracing tracks and taxied to the front of the grandstand. El Lobo had a snatch of hay fifteen minutes after takeoff.

Flying flowers. National Skyways airflifted its first Southern California crop of Christmas poinsettias, grown by horticulturist Paul Ecke, on December 2, 1945. Columbia Pictures' Ann Miller (right) handing over a potted plant of poinsettias to Flying Tiger Camille Joseph 'Joe' Rosbert (left) at Long Beach Municipal airport before its takeoff to Chicago. Florist Clarence Brown is in the centre. The Budd's cargo hold could carry 8,000 pounds of poinsettias. Columbia Pictures

First West-East commercial air shipment of furniture. With chaise longue and ottoman tucked under his arms, a freight handler is loading solid aluminum furniture made by Deeco Inc in Los Angeles into the hold of a Conestoga on the first west to east commercial air shipment of furniture. It was flying to Chicago for display at the first postwar furniture market which opened in February 1946. In contrast to the lightweight aluminium furniture, other cargo was a pair of electronic high-frequency heaters, weighing 660 pounds each, destined for Detroit, Michigan for use at a convention of the Society of Plastic Engineers.

Velvet Horns, a thoroughbred mare owned by orchestra leader Harry James, was believed to be the first horse transported by air, in order that she might reach her home ranch in time to give birth. Arrangements for flying her from San Diego to Burbank with National Skyways were made by the Blood Stock Agency. Robert P. 'Duke' Hedman, with sunglasses and Bill Bartling on the left of Duke are watching the unload of the precious cargo.

The Budd RB-1s gave way to the Douglas C-47s in 1946. The first C-47s originally carried National Skyway Freight titles on the nose section. Captain Camille Joseph 'Joe' Rosbert is in the centre and on the right is Captain Robert P. Hedman, vice-president of operations.

The wartime shark insignia was carried on to this peacetime Flying Tiger Line Douglas C-47. Otto Rothschild

First airborne lumber to Texas. Probably the strangest-looking Flying Tiger plane ever to fly was this Flying Tiger Line Douglas C-47-DL NC59277 which Maurice Angly, a wealthy Texas lumberman, chartered to bring 5,000 pounds of hand-picked Douglas fir paneling from Portland Columbia airport to Galveston on April 4, 1946. Angly named it the Thunderbird, and had the Walt Disney studios in Hollywood decorate the aircraft to resemble the mythical bird which tops the totem poles of Indian tribes in Alaska and the Pacific Northwest. The aircraft was flown by Captain Herbert J. Wall who used to fly 'the Hump' in China, and by Captain Mack McKay, acting co-pilot, late of the Fifth Air Force.

First shipment of furniture airlifted from Los Angeles to Cincinnati in May 1946. The banner on the aircraft has the name of John Shillito Co, Cincinnati's first department store founded in 1830 and commonly known as Shillito's. Otto Rothschild

First race horses to fly out of Mexico City. Four horses including Jackstraw, Polotico and Tupinamba were flown in 1946 from Mexico City to the Arlington Park racecourse in Chicago aboard NC18927, a Flying Tiger Line C-47 equipped with four horse stalls.

British-born actor Leslie Townes 'Bob' Hope, with Norma Deloris Egstrom, known professionally as Peggy Lee, an American jazz and popular music singer, songwriter, composer, and actress, on the tarmac in front of a Flying Tigers C-47 after the arrival of 3,000 copies of Bob's latest record, I Never Left Home (Capitol Records). A sign on the plane reads, Flying Tiger Special: Loaded With Hope.   Gene Lester

Elsie visits California. Before Joe Camel, before the Energizer Bunny... 'Bovine glamour' reigned in the form of Elsie the cow, famous spokescow for the Borden Milk Company. Elsie arrived on a Flying Tiger Line C-47 early October 1946 to be a guest of the San Mateo Fiesta. Rosemary LaPlanche, on the left, wartime Miss America and film star, joined the welcome party.

Cargo for Sears. Robert Prescott in good company in front of a Douglas C-47 fully loaded with garments and women's clothing for Sears. Otto Rothschild

A replacement for the Budd. Between 1946 and 1948, Flying Tigers relied heavily on the Douglas C-47, the cargo version of the famed DC-3. A replacement for the Budd Conestoga, the C-47 could fly 7,500 pounds of cargo over a range of 600 miles at 150 miles per hour. Flying Tigers operated 11 C-47s which flew Roy Rogers' wonder horse Trigger, homeward-bound sailors, Elsie the Borden Cow, silverware, funiture, flowers and anything else that would fit through the airport gate. Top picture is C-47-DL NC59277 carrying National Skyways titles on the nose and Flying Tiger Line titles on the fuselage. Note the Tiger shark logo on the rear fuselage. Bottom picture is C-47A NC64747 carrying additional California Furniture Fashions and Chicago Here We Come titles.

Originally built for the USAAF in November 1942, Flying Tiger Line Douglas C-47 NC18927 was acquired in December 1945 and flew for the airline until October 1949, and seen here at Burbank.

Douglas C-47A NC63164 at Burbank around 1947, with unusual Flying Tiger Transport titles and large FTT markings under the wing. The aircraft was acquired by National Skyways in 1946 and flew for two years before being sold to India. This is the oldest colour document in the Flying Tigers Club archives.

The first Flying Tiger Line office, on Hollywood Way and Empire Avenue in Burbank, in 1947.   Lloyd Sherman

The Flying Tiger Line Inc.

GENERAL OFFICES: LOCKHEED AIR TERMINAL   BURBANK, CALIF.   STANLEY 7-3411

UNITED STATES AIRFREIGHT ROUTE NO. 100   CABLE ADDRESS: FLYTIGER

Gregory 'Pappy' Boyington, Marine air ace and former member of Chennault's Flying Tigers, had plans to join the Flying Tiger Line in Burbank, as sales representative on their worldwide routes in July 1947, but these never materialised in the end.

First of the four-engine propliners. In 1946, Tigers won a lucrative contract from Air Transport Command to supply the American Occupation forces in Japan. Thus began the largest, longest airlift ever flown by a private contractor. Through 1947, 32 Douglas C-54s flew 28 weekly flights between the United States, Hawaii and Tokyo. The Tigers flew the contract for almost a year, proving for all time that the airline was capable of providing a major airfreight operation over a sustained period of time. Upon completion of this airlift, the C-54 continued as the backbone of the Tigers' domestic and international operations. The C-54 was able to airlift 19,840 pounds of cargo, cruised at 210 miles per hour, and had a range of 2,000 miles.

Douglas C-54G NC90911 during a stop in Honolulu during the Korean war, with an all metallic livery and Flying Tiger Line titles.

Douglas C-54B NC67548 in its first full Flying Tiger Line colours in Burbank. The aircraft joined the fleet in 1946 and flew with the airline until 1954.
Lloyd Sherman

Shipper's Safety. Robert Prescott, president of the Flying Tiger Line, left, demonstrates the new sealed security safeguards used by his company for the protection of airfreight shippers on a newly delivered C-54 in October 1947. Sealed security enables the company to call in the FBI if the seal is broken by an unauthorised person. Pilot O. Trapp, centre, holds a pouch of seals. Vern C. Miller of the carrier's security division is at right. Lloyd Sherman

A new record was established by the Flying Tiger Line in 1947, when 40,000 day-old chicks flew from Hayward Municipal airport by C-47 on a one and a half hour trip to Oxnard. The flight was the largest single order of baby chicks and the largest number ever flown by plane, valued at $10,000. The 6 Watson Bros. Photography Inc.

Douglas C-54D NC91083 in its first Flying Tiger Line colours in Burbank. The aircraft was leased from the USAF in 1948 and flew with the airline until 1954.

The last Budd leaves with most of the crew who worked on the ship originally on hand to say goodbye. Left to right, standing, Jim Duehren, Joe Baker, Bob Ghormley, Paul Grace, Buck Buchanan, Bob Norton, Leon Pryate (Colly) Colquette, Jack Studer, Al Goldberg; front row, left to right, Bill Thompson, Art Lawson, Rhuel Trimble, Joe Cuppett and Joe Gwynn. Few were sorry to see the ungainly Budds depart.

A veteran returns. 1949 marked the return of a trusted friend and familiar veteran. The Curtiss C-46 Commando that many Tigers flew on supply missions over the Hump during World War II, came home for civilian duty. The C-46 Commando was the largest twin-engine aircraft of its day. Its 200 miles per hour speed, 13,000 pounds cargo capacity, and 900 mile range made it the queen of the Tiger fleet. A total of 42 C-46s were operated by the Flying Tiger Line. The first were delivered in late 1949, followed by 25 leased from the USAF. Flying Tigers was able to put them to good use within the United States as the airlift of men and material across the Pacific to Korea began to use all available long range C-54s. Most of these C-46s were purchased outright within a very few years. Pictured are three C-46s lined up on the Flying Tiger Line ramp at home base in Burbank.

Celebrating the U.S. Air Freight Route 100 certificate. 1949 was the year that the Civil Aeronautics Board awarded Flying Tiger Line the first transcontinental all-cargo Freight Route 100. During a board of directors party to celebrate, Robert Prescott is holding a gag newspaper titled "Tigers Certificated! AAL-UAL Junk Fleet!". A provisional certificate was issued in May 1947 followed by a five year certificate in July 1949. Some of the executives and their spouses including, left to right, Norman L. Meyers; Helen Ruth Prescott, third from the left; Ester Benninger, seventh from the left looking down the newspaper; Fred Benninger, at the rear with glasses; William (Bill) E. Bartling; Samuel (Sam) B. Mosher; Robert Prescott, holding the newspaper; George T. Cussen, rear between Bob and Sam; Cynthia Bartling, front holding a glass; Allen T. Chase; and Catherine Meyers, far right and holding a glass.

Bill Bauler

Long Beach May 1949, Robert W. Prescott and Helen Ruth Prescott holding the first US all cargo scheduled Route 100 certificate at the crew door of a C-54 together with a group of employees. As a result of the route, new stations were opened in Oakland, Denver, Milwaukee, Toledo, Akron-Canton, Buffalo, Rochester, Philadelphia, Hartford, Providence, and Boston.

First day as a certified transcontinental cargo carrier. The inaugural ceremony at the Billy Mitchell Field, now Milwaukee Mitchell International, on October 18, 1949 marked the Flying Tiger Line's first day as a certified transcontinental cargo carrier. It included adding the name Sky Tiger Milwaukee by Frank W. Greusel, chairman of the Air Service Bureau of the Milwaukee Association of Commerce.

The Flying Tiger Line inaugural flight out of Burbank on October 18, 1949 was made with Douglas C-54G N90911 and shown with one of the early freight loads.

Planeload of kentias. The first full planeload of palms to be shipped without special packing or containers, but loaded on a freight car, was received by Frank Oeschslin & Co, of Cicero Illinois, from the Bassett & Washburn Kentia Nurseries, Sierra Madre, California. No racks or special equipment was used. The interior of the Flying Tigers Curtiss C-46 used for that charter was lined with burlap in order that the palms would not come in contact with the metal sheathing of the plane and risk being damaged by cold at high altitude. The pilots were instructed to maintain a temperature of 45 degrees in the cargo compartment while in transit and not to exceed 16,000 feet in altitude while in flight. The 10,240 pounds load of palms, not wrapped but in paper pots, were stacked on the floor of the C-46, two tiers high and held in place by cargo belts.

Douglas C-54D N91071 was leased to the Flying Tiger Line by the USAF in 1949. Soon after, Associated Airways was founded by Dick Rossi as a non-scheduled passenger airline, operating the aircraft to Honolulu in Flying Tiger livery with Associated Airways titles. One of the first stewardess Rossi hired was Frances 'Fran' Drew, who later joined the Flying Tiger Line and became a celebrity spokesperson for airline until 1957. The aircraft is seen in Burbank around 1949. Lloyd Sherman

Flying Tiger Line C-54B N86581 during a layover at Andersen Air Force Base, Guam in early 1950 on an Air Transport Command flight.
Jacques Guillem Collection

Tokyo airlift. Pasadena Star-News Aviation Editor Don Downie, right, and Captain Ed Pinke check their instruments in a Flying Tiger Line C-54 before departing for Tokyo with a load of troops in September 1950, routing via Honolulu and Wake Island. The Star-News arranged a jumpseat for Downie on this flight, to bring Star-News readers the story of the Tiger Pacific airlift.

Downie and Associates

Onboard a Flying Tiger Line C-54 flying to Tokyo, Yanks whiling away the time in standard Army fashion – a round of poker.

Don Downie

Refuelling in Tokyo. Don Downie

End of the line. Back from Tokyo after a 13,000 mile Pacific Airlift on a Flying Tiger Line C-54, Captain Ed Pinke, left, and Star-News Aviation Editor Don Downie, carry their bags into the flight operations office at Burbank.   Downie and Associates

Oriental Seamen board plane for home. 51 oriental crew members of the British tramp freighter John Lyras, who refused to leave San Diego harbour with the ship due to its military cargo, instead boarded Flying Tiger Line C-54G N90910 on October 12, 1950, flying home to Bombay (today Mumbai). Colourfully attired in turbans, fez-type headwear, berets, and sun helmets, the seamen included 38 Muslim Indians, 12 Roman Catholic Goanese (Portuguese) Indians; and one Chinese. They first objected to sailing because they believed the vessel was bound for Korea. When told by the Indian consul general in San Francisco that the craft was headed for Japan, they continued to insist on being sent home. Shown at top of plane (under the command of Captain Howard F. Brooks) is Hal Ramsden, local station manager of the Flying Tiger Line. The plane came back on October 17 with 51 replacement crewmembers.

Korea gift lift. During the Air Transportation Day festivities at Los Angeles on Sunday November 12, 1950, the Flying Tiger Line had a C-46 on display and organised a collection of gifts for GIs based in Korea. Sultry screen actress Susan Hayward, honorary chairperson of the Los Angeles Junior Chamber of Commerce's Operation Gift Lift, was on hand to accept Christmas gifts for shipment to servicemen in Korea. Co-pilot Frank Otey on left and Captain Jack Morris on right took also took part in the air fete. Photos William Eccles

Christmas party December 1950. First five-year employee group during the Christmas party of December 1950 in Burbank. First row, left to right, 'Duke' Hedman, Art Lawson, Paul Grace, Joe Cuppett, Helen Ruth Prescott, Rhuel Trimble, Mayo Thomas. Second row: 'Red' Duehren, Bob Ghormley, Joe Baker, Ed Hembree, Leon 'Colly' Colquette, Cordell 'Buck' Buchanan, Charlotte Waltz, Robert Prescott, Herb Wall and Jim Jackson.

Paul E. Wolfe

Air network design. Robert Prescott marking up on the blackboard in 1951.

Graphic House, Inc.

Their majesties ride high. Dog day farewell in March 1951 on a Flying Tiger Line plane, when 21 prize canines were loaded aboard in Burbank to fly to Madison Square Gardens in New York for a dog show. Value of the dog cargo exceeded $25,000, and here are some of the champions before the long transcontinental trip. From left to right, Champion Marques Ar For, wire-haired terrier; Champion Pied Piper, red and white cocker; Champion Tiger Tail Gay Pilot, black cocker who was Best of Breed. (The Boxer puppy was a "stowaway.") In the foreground, J. B. Hickey, veteran dog handler, who accompanied the dogs, poses with Champion Staber's Inspiration, a pointer, and a "girlfriend."

Paul E. Wolfe

Nurse Duke. Burbank hangar April 1951. One of the busiest spots in the hangar at Burbank was the First Aid Room. R. N. Duke, more familiarly known as Nurse Duke to all of the employees, was in charge. Nurse Duke was the first Flying Tiger Line nurse (and a good one), hired on January 7, 1947. It was not an easy position, in as much as Duke was on call 24 hours a day. Nurse Duke was later assisted by clerical assistant, Edna Avery. In addition to first aid treatment, and rushing the seriously wounded to a doctor, Nurse Duke administered shots to overseas personnel. This consisted of a series of five, for typhoid, smallpox, typhus and cholera, with booster shots every six months. She gave as many as twenty to thirty shots daily, and the monthly average was around 250.

A group of early cabin crew pose in front of Curtiss C-46F N67995 in 1951 at Burbank. From left to right are unknown, Fran Drew, Billie Welsh and unknown. Billie Welsh was Flying Tiger Line first chief flight attendant until she resigned in November 1951 to be wed.

Flying Tigers flight attendant Frances 'Fran' Drew during a photo shoot in 1951 with Military Air Transport personnel exiting a Douglas C-54 during the Korean airlift. This series of pictures was taken in Burbank by Peter A. Gowland, famous glamour photographer and actor. He shot more than 1,000 magazine covers, mostly glamour shots of female models but also portraits of celebrities.

Fran Drew always seemed to attract military personnel. A former fashion model and entertainer in the chorus line on the Earl Carroll Show, she became a Flying Tiger Line flight attendant in 1951 where she was selected to do public relations activities. She was a celebrity spokesperson for the company from 1951 to 1957 as well as a senior flight attendant. She wrote a novel called Tale Of The Tiger in 1981.

Peter A. Gowland

Operation Wetback. Starting in July 1951, struggling through the early unprofitable days of airfreight, the Flying Tiger Line managed to survive by flying charters for the military, tourist groups and the U.S. Immigration Service. Four Tiger Curtiss C-46 aircraft returned illegal Mexican immigrants to Guadalajara, Mexico, from the borders of California and Texas.

Wetback charter flights, as they were referred to in those days, were flown deep into Mexico to cities like Mazatlán, San Luis Potosí, Guadalajara and Durango, each being over 300 miles from the United States - Mexico border. Immigration authorities hoped the distance would discourage a quick return of the deported Mexicans to the US.

Curtiss C-46F N67977 at the Flying Tiger hangar terminal, Newark, New Jersey circa 1951.

Glad to be here. Forty Russian refugees from China wave as they deplane from a Flying Tiger Douglas C-54 which brought them from Manila to San Francisco on July 28, 1951. The group fled before the Communist advance in China and were given asylum in the Philippines before coming to the United States under a special act of Congress. The aircraft was under the command of Captain Dick Rossi.   Ken McLaughlin

A Flying Tiger Line C-46 aircraft arrived at Oakland municipal airport on September 5, 1951 with a group of British war brides with their American youngsters; and 38 University of California students returning after an 80-day air trip through Europe. For a bargain $995, they visited Denmark, Sweden, Germany, Austria, Switzerland, Italy, France, Spain, The Netherlands, Britain and North Africa.

On December 7, 1951, the new office building in Burbank was officially dedicated; the flag was raised at the beginning of the programme. Helen Ruth Prescott, first wife of Robert Prescott, attached the commemorative plaque to the building. Prescott and various other officials from the CAA and Chambers of Commerce gave short speeches. Open House followed in the flower-bedecked building. December 7, 1941 was a day of infamy for the United States. Conversely, for the Flying Tiger Line, December 7, 1951 was a day of demonstration of American pride.

Christmas party December 1951. From left to right are Captain Dick Rossi, Captain Bill Pattison and Stewardess Fran Drew. The ratio of cups to people was overwhelming!

Jack Birns

Curtiss C-46F N67981 in pristine condition at Flying Tigers' Burbank base.

A shipment of blood for soldiers in Korea is loaded aboard a Flying Tigers C-46 freighter at Burbank in February 1952, after delivery by the Red Cross. The blood was then flown to Travis Air Force Base, north of San Francisco, where it was loaded on a Flying Tiger Pacific Air Lift C-54 freighter bound for Tokyo.

Flying heifers. On March 20, 1952, one hundred head of dairy calves were flown from Milwaukee to Lynchburg for placement on farms. All one hundred, consisting of 83 Holsteins, nine Brown Swiss and eight Guernseys, were on a single Flying Tiger C-46. The project was considered unique in the dairy states of the Midwest. Milwaukee Journal Picture

Flying Tiger Line C-54G N90910 at Honolulu airport around 1952, still sporting the basic livery of previous operator Resort Airlines. Don Downie

"A convenient way to get it to the West Coast" said George D. Webber, president of Webber Gage Co. in May 1952, who sent his slow-slung Jaguar to Los Angeles three times by Flying Tiger Line, coast to coast. George was parking his car at the Cleveland airport before boarding an airliner heading west, and with luck, his car would be there for him to drive away, thus solving the airport to town transportation problem.

Between 1952 and 1956, the Flying Tiger Line ran ad campaigns with comic book style cartoons in mainstream magazines such as Business Week, Time, the New Yorker, the Wall Street Journal and Aviation Week.

Lockheed Air Terminal setting for the first annual reunion of the AVG Flying Tigers. With Claire Lee Chennault (centre right), Flying Tigers gathered at Burbank for a TV and photo moment in June 1952. In the background is Curtiss P-40N Warhawk NL1195N. Originally delivered to the RCAF in 1942, it flew in the 2000 movie Pearl Harbor and was still airworthy in 2023.

Claire Lee Chennault (centre) and Marilyn Maxwell at Burbank next to Curtiss P-40N Warhawk NL1195N during the AVG Flying Tigers first reunion in June 1952. Maxwell was a famed actress and entertainer. In a career that spanned the 1940s and 1950s, she appeared in several films and radio programs, and entertained the troops during World War II and the Korean War on United Service Organizations (USO) tours with Bob Hope. Coy Watson

Together at Burbank on the steps of a C-54 with six month-old tiger cub 'Toungoo', mascot-to-be of the Flying Tigers first reunion in June 1952, are stewardess Skip Lawson; in her arms are Marilyn Haywood and Suzanne Haywood (left), daughters of Captain Tom Haywood, one of the original Flying Tigers AVG.   Coy Watson

Claire Lee Chennault (centre), organiser and leader of the Flying Tigers combat squadron is being "taxied" into the Santa Monica Swimming Club on June 28, 1952, aboard a rickshaw pulled by members of his original group. Captain Dick Rossi is on the front right. Host at the Flying Tigers' party honouring General and Mrs Chennault was Douglas Aircraft Co.

On October 1, 1952, the Flying Tiger Line dispatched its first Curtiss C-46 aircraft to inaugurate cargo service under US Navy contract. This contract called for daily service from Oakland, San Francisco, Los Angeles and San Diego to Norfolk, New York, Philadelphia and Washington. The first flight departed Oakland with Miss Jayne Devereux acting as mistress of ceremonies. At the same time, a similar flight was departing from Washington, DC westbound.

Jet freighter. In early October 1952, a tiny jet pod was installed under the belly of Tiger C-46F N67979 and tested. With both props feathered, the plane was able to sustain level flight relying on the power of a single French-built 299 pound Marbore II turbojet. The photo was taken was from another C-46F, N67988.

Bill R. Watson

The C-46 cockpit provided space for two pilots and a radio operator. The 25 or so instruments were in four panels, each easily removable. Access to the plumbing and wiring behind the panels was facilitated by the removable nose cone.　　　　　　　　　　　　　　　　　　　　　　Bill R. Watson

Ditching training. Captain Jack F. Morris is assisting a Flying Tiger Line stewardess with her life vest, as part of crew emergency ditching training in October 1952 near the Hansen Dam in the San Fernando Valley, California.

Christmas party December 1952. Robert Prescott with Tiger Girl Lee Wilson in his arms. On the right and back are George T. Cussen together with Bill Bartling. Bandleader and tenor saxophonist Frederick 'Freddy" A. Martin is at left. The party was held at the Hollywood Palladium on December 17 when more than 2,000 Tigers and guests took over the night club for their holiday event. Bill R. Watson

Short-lived first Constellation. In January 1953, the Flying Tiger Line intended to lease a Lockheed L-049 Constellation from Intercontinental Airlines for use on military contract flights. The aircraft was destroyed in a training accident on January 22, 1953 prior to delivery. (It had been scheduled to pick up its first passengers at Oakland the next day.) N38936 was built in 1943, the second Constellation for the USAF, and made a record-breaking flight on April 17, 1944, from the Lockheed Air Terminal to Washington DC, piloted by Jack Frye and Howard Hughes in full TWA colours and markings with The Transcontinental Line titling, but with USAAF serial number. It is seen here at Burbank a few days before the accident sporting 'chartered by The Flying Tiger Line' titles.

The L-049 Constellation N38936 made an inadvertent gear-up landing during an acceptance test flight on January 22, 1953. The circuit-breaker on the system that would have given warning of 'undercarriage up' had been disconnected, which the pilots had forgotten to reconnect, and a perfect wheels-up landing made. The crew of ten escaped uninjured, but fuel valves were left open and the aircraft was quickly enveloped by flames. Onboard were Senior Pilot C. G. Fredericks; Larry Raab, Sheldon Eichel, August Martin and Leo Gardner, all pilots; Radio Operator Morris Sherry; CAA Inspectors Sam Chandler and M. H. Griffith; Flight Engineer Frank Lutomski, and Robert Jackson. None of the crewmembers aboard the gear up landing were Tiger pilots. The next morning revealed the severity of the wreck on the runway of Burbank airport.

A New York Airways Sikorsky S-55, N406A, is sitting next to a Flying Tiger Line C-46F at Newark Airport around 1953. N406A is one of New York Airways' original batch of S-55s, delivered in late October 1952. Note the Skybus title beneath the cabin windows.

Onloading a cargo load of Tuffy dishwashing products with a Towmotor fork lift aboard Curtiss C-46F N67958.

San Fernando Valley Airport open house. Tiger Girl Lee Wilson, mascot of the Flying Tiger Line, joins Captain Tom Haywood on May 16, 1953 on the steps of Douglas C-54G N90911 on static display at the third annual San Fernando Valley Airport open house.

Bill R. Watson

Tiger Girl Lee Wilson, mascot of the Flying Tiger Line joins Tommy Haywood, chief pilot on the Korean run, in the cockpit of of Douglas C-54G N90911 on display at the third annual San Fernando Valley Airport open house on May 17, 1953.   Bill R. Watson

Slick Airways Douglas DC-6A N90810 'Miss Judy' at the Burbank's carrier base in 1953 while leased to the Flying Tiger Line, still in Slick livery.
Jon Proctor Collection

90 Korea veterans returned from overseas duty are grouped on the loading ramp before boarding Flying Tiger Line DC-6A N90810 (leased from Slick Airways) at Oakland airport in early July 1953. The destination is Camp Kilmer, New Jersey, for discharges or leaves. This is believed to be largest single group of returning vets flown by a domestic airline. They were among 1,000 men flown out of Oakland by 19 planes of the Independent Military Air Transport Association and the Air Coach Transport Association, under charter to the Army and the Air Force, to transport servicemen to separation centres. Richard Muller

Damaged in take-off crack-up. Flying Tiger Line C-46F N67992, en route for Burbank loaded with automotive parts, was damaged on July 31, 1953 at Salt Lake Municipal Airport. Pilot James L. Bledsoe reported the plane was not going to clear the north end of the runway on the take-off roll. He applied the 'blinders' that lock the large wheels of the craft. The tires blew out as the plane skidded, finally nosing over into a fence after skidding for nearly 100 yards along the runway. The plane then righted itself. No fire developed and after damages were estimated, the aircraft was repaired. The other two Tiger crew members onboard were R. E. Corey, co-pilot, and James L. Cullen.

Interplanetary airfreight. Flying Tiger developed an "authentic" flying saucer in 1952 that was used for several promotion stunts. Pictured is blonde Tiger Girl Leigh Snowden with a pair of dwarfs in front of the Emporium department store on Market Street in San Francisco on October 30, 1953. The contraption, brainchild of the engineers of the Flying Tiger Line, attracted a lot of attention!

Unusual air cargo. Next to Flying Tiger Line Douglas DC-4 N30058 at Burbank are two California Glasspar fiberglass-body sports.
Bill R. Watson

Seeking globe-girdling record. Dianna C. Bixby and her de Havilland DH.98 Mosquito N1203V named Miss Flying Tiger at Burbank in April 1954. Dianna was going to fly around the world from San Francisco, via Newark, Paris, Basra, Karachi, Calcutta, Tokyo, Midway Island, and back to San Francisco. In April 16, 1954, the Mosquito roared out of San Francisco on the way to Newark. Somewhere along her route, she ran into bad weather and technical problems which caused her to abandon the whole effort. Dianna later lost her life on January 2, 1955 when her twin-engine Douglas A-20 Havoc bomber Serial 43-22217 crashed into the sea in bad weather off Loreto, Baja California. She was 32. Bill R. Watson

Delivered new to the Flying Tiger Line in March 1954, DC-6A N34959 is readied for its next scheduled flight. Bill R. Watson

Flying Tiger facilities at Burbank, California, which were planned to be integrated with Slick Airways. The Flying Tiger office is just outside the airport directly above the Flying Tiger hangar.

Robert Young

Flying Tiger - Slick merger. A Tiger-Slick 'knot-tying' merger ceremony was held on May 12, 1954 at Burbank. Robert Prescott, right, and Tommy L. Grace, president of Slick Airways, left, united to create the world's largest air freight line. Centre is Mary "Kaki" Whitney, "Miss World Trade." Named Flying Tiger-Slick Airlines, the new company had a fleet of 53 aircraft on the nation's largest domestic route system, serving 45 major marketing and manufacturing centres. Nearly 3,000 people attended the official ceremonies at the Lockheed Air Terminal in Burbank. Flying Tigers and Slick Airways got a divorce in September 1954, blaming labour problems. Founded by Earl Slick in 1946, the airline was shut down in 1966 due to its poor financial situation, and its assets were acquired by Airlift International.

Peanuts the circus clown, and Frances Clark, animal trainer, bid farewell to Tessie, a nine-month-old 250 pound Indian elephant, as she leaves by Flying Tiger-Slick DC-6 at Burbank, for Saint Louis in late May 1954. This baby elephant was a gift from the Maharajah of Nepal to August A. Busch, noted sportsman, for his famous game collection at Grant's Farm, near Saint Louis.

Miss World Trade. Mary Katherine Whitney, Miss World Trade, who was one of the guests at the Open House and merger ceremonies, has just returned in May 1954 from a flight around the world to "sell" Southern California's trade to a dozen foreign markets. Mary, a stewardess with Pan American World Airways, flew via Flying Tiger-Slick air freighter from Lockheed Air Terminal, Burbank to New York, and the flight continued via Pan American Clipper. Bill R. Watson

During the short-lived Flying Tiger-Slick marriage, a handful of aircraft were painting with dual titles such as C-46F N4875V which entered service in July 1954 and is seen here at Burbank.
Bill R. Watson

The Burbank's sheet metal shop mechanics. Burbank, August 1954, from left to right, standing are Bill Cashon, Anderson, unknown, Jack McLarty, Carlini, Tim Tammius, Johnny Koffer, unknown, unknown, unknown, Bill Collies, unknown, Harry Moreno, Winnie Lasko, unknown, Don Savage, Berry Sudderth, Joe Margadona and Willy Skaggs. Kneeling are unknown, unknown, Al Cormier, Phillips, Scheaffer, unknown, unknown, Hawkins, Rauel Berrigan, unknown, and Allen Lee.

Flying Tiger Line DC-4 N88940 at London Airport on a rainy day.

Jon Proctor Collection

The Los Angeles Times. In January 1955, more than 5,000 traffic and shipping executives throughout the world received copies of the Los Angeles Times Midwinter edition. Supervising the loading of the papers on the Los Angeles ramp in front of the Pan Am hangar are, from left, Harry Heflin, Midwinter edition advertising manager; George Cussen, vice president of the Flying Tiger Line, and Harold T. Miller of the Port of Los Angeles. Pan Am distributed the Times westbound and Flying Tiger eastbound.

A Flying Tiger C-54 arrives at Burbank from the east with a full load of freight.

Meeting distraction. El Rancho Vegas model Cynthia Brooks was elected Miss Flying Tiger in February 1955 for a meeting organised by the California Funeral Directors Association. Besides posing for pictures, Cynthia's purpose at the meeting was to inform the group that Flying Tigers carried more air freight than any other airline but there is a belief that most of the boys attending the meeting forgot the message. The El Rancho Vegas was a hotel and casino at the north end of the Las Vegas Strip in Winchester, Nevada. It opened in 1941, as the first resort on the Strip. Desert Sea News Bureau Las Vegas, Nevada

The DEW Line. In early 1955, Flying Tiger Line made the largest single contribution of any carrier to the vast Distant Early Warning Line, also known as the DEW Line, the building of the North American radar fence across Canada, high up in the Arctic Circle. The performance of flight crews and ground personnel, in true pioneering conditions, was exceptional, and resulted in the company moving the largest freight volume of any operator engaged in the project. Almost five and a half million pounds of freight were carried, and miles flown exceeded 700,000. Flying Tiger deployed Curtiss C-46Fs and C-54s, including C-54D N4890V

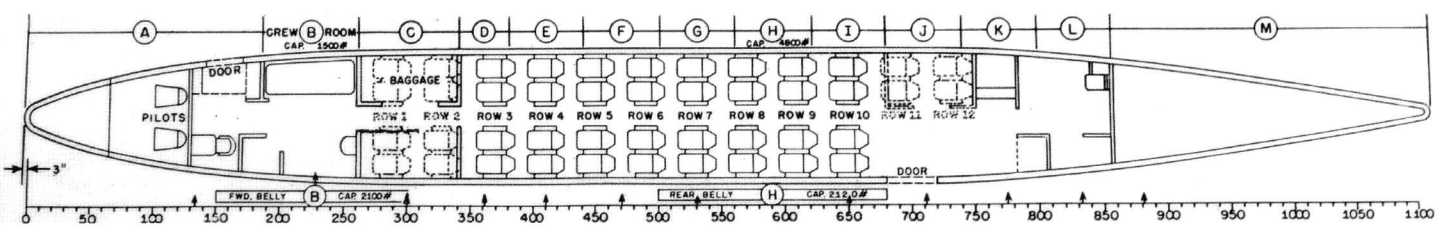

Passengers are boarding Flying Tiger Line Douglas C-54A N56010 at New York Idlewild.

Photo by Enell, Inc. N.Y. International Airport

Starting a 14-nation peace tour of Asia and the Middle East, the first contingent of a 177-member mission of the Moral Re-Armanent Association, an international moral and spiritual movement, left Lockheed Air Terminal on June 12, 1955 on chartered Flying Tiger C-54. First stop was Tokyo.

Flying Tiger Line 10th anniversary. Mary Ann McHenry, Flying Tiger Girl, waits for a slice of cake along with Mayor George Vermillion (centre) as Robert Prescott does the honours. The luncheon was held in the second-floor restaurant of the administration building of the Long Beach airport on June 24, 1955. The Flying Tiger Line was founded in Long Beach on June 25, 1945.

A commemorative plaque marking the tenth anniversary of the Flying Tiger Line was put in place on June 24, 1955 at Long Beach Municipal Airport, with the help of Mary Ann McHenry, Flying Tiger Girl and Lakewood Miss California entry, Robert Prescott, and Mayor George Vermillion of Long Beach, next to RP on the right.

Burbank's mechanics doing an inspection job on a Douglas C-54, fleet number 410, up on jacks inside the maintenance hangar. The hangar could accomodate two C-54s, usually parked face to face.

Shipment of thoroughbred racehorses brought the Flying Tiger Line some of the best publicity.

Vacations at minimum expense. Washington, D.C. August 1955. the Civil Aeronautics Club, made up of Civil Aeronautics Board and Civil Aeronautics Administration employees, launched a new idea in flying vacations for government workers when they boarded a Flying Tiger DC-6 at Washington, D.C., bound for London and Brussels. The revised CAB policy on overseas passenger charters enabled club members and their families to charter Flying Tiger Line aircraft at a cost of $260 per person for a round trip to Europe. Club president Harry Pickering predicted that the idea would, "soon be adopted by many other government agencies because it provided wonderful vacations at minimum expense."

Inauguration of the first all-freight service to the twin cities of Minneapolis and Saint Paul on September 15, 1955. Here is the Tiger crew on hand for the inaugural flight (left to right standing) John Higgins, BUR; Frank Connolly, EWR; George T. Cussen, BUR; Robert Prescott, BUR (with Ed Trott just behind him); Frank Clain, CHI; Captain Ed Lowe; Mrs. Marie Haywood, mother of Captain Tom Haywood; Mrs. Mary Haywood, aunt of Tom; Mayo Thomas, BUR: Pete Albert, BUR; Paul Ohman, Minneapolis-St. Paul trucker; Woodie Woodward, BUR; Bob Blanks, SFO; Frank Siwicki, CHI; kneeling left to right: Chuck Shumway BUR; Bob Steel, MSP; Vernon Gray, PHL; George Mildeberger, BGM; Len Kimball, BUR.   Philip C. Dittes

Crew preparation at San Francisco. With night fall, freight begins to roll through the San Francisco station and crews arrive for the first flights. Here co-pilot Don Van Handel (left) and Captain Dick Rossi look over a flight clearance for the first of two sections to Burbank.

Captain A. Perrault (left) signs the flight clearance prepared by First Officer Joe A. Merlo for the second section to Burbank.

Arrival in San Francisco. Busiest part of the night is the arrival of flight 251 from Detroit. This Douglas DC-6A managed a fast two hour, 45 minute turnaround on a rainy January 1956 night, with gas trucks and fork lifts on the job.

Captain John D. "Woody" Woodward lugs his bags to the station after flying the 251 into San Francisco from Romulus Michigan, later Detroit-Wayne County.

The Oakland station in late 1955 was located across the bay from the San Francisco station and housed in this quonset building.

Flying submarine. The Flying Tiger Line would have bet its collective shirts that they would never see a submarine on an aircraft. And they would have lost in February 1956, when a submarine flew on a Flying Tiger C-54, yet another first in air transport history. Manufactured by Aero-Jet General Company of Azusa California, makers of missiles, jet equipment, etc., it was the answer to any skindiver's dream, $6,000 at the time. Dubbed the Mini Sub, it was designed for underwater fishing. This one was destined for Bermuda when it was loaded on the Daybreaker flight at Burbank. Pictured are (left to right) Bernard Tenney, Burbank District Sales Manager; Tiger girl, Ann Gill of Burbank Sales; W. H. Taft, of Aero-Jet publicity, and C. A. Gongwer, head of Aero Jet's underwater division.

Army GIs on a 30 day furlough are all smiles as they leave on a chartered Flying Tigers C-54 from Frankfurt for the Statue of Liberty. Stewardess Fran Drew is in the back of the plane next to the door. The American Legion sponsored the trip. Richart Muller

Douglas DC-6A N34959 was delivered new in March 1954 and flew for Tigers as a convertible passenger/freight aircraft until May 1958. After a long career in several airlines in the US and Canada, it flew last with Everts Air Cargo, named Good Grief, until 2016, and made its short final flight from Fairbanks to Chena Hot Springs Airport on October 2, 2016 and is displayed atop three large steel pylons.

Jacques Guillem Collection

Elmer, a 496 pounds baby African elephant, arrived at Seattle Boeing Field from New York on the last lap of her journey from British East Africa on Flying Tiger flight 361 on June 14, 1956. With her were Frank Vincenzi (not pictured), chief trainer of Seattle's Woodland Park Zoo, and Pearl Steves, Miss Flying Tiger. Olin E. Myers

Two-year-old Elmer had two traveling companions, a pair of cheetahs, in which she showed absolutely no interest and for their part, even the cheetahs seem rather nonchalant about beautiful Pearl Steves, Miss Flying Tiger.　　Olin E. Myers

Air Express shipments began moving on Flying Tiger Line flights for the first time on June 11, 1956. At Seattle, Richard M. Einar, general agent for the Railway Express Agency and Air Express, hands the first shipment to Flying Tiger Girl, Pearl Steves, representing the airline in Seattle's Miss Air Power contest.

The scene shown above was a daily or nightly routine at New York for the Flying Tiger Line. The Bremervoerder Choir group flew by Douglas C-54 to Europe and back in summer 1956, out to Bremen on July 15 and back on August 18.   Aviation News

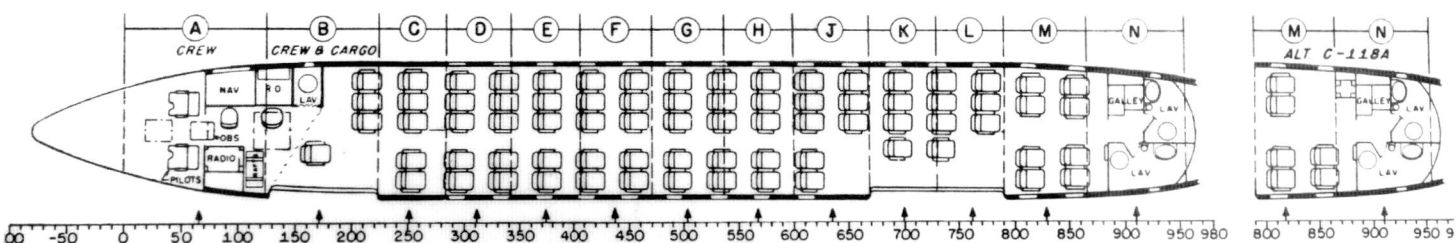

A typical North Atlantic travel group, military personnel, their wives and children bound to Frankfurt, Germany in July 1956, all aboard a high-density, yet comfortable Flying Tiger Line flagship Douglas DC-6 accommodating 100 passengers. The flight had departed from New York International, where the Flying Tiger Line headquartered their North Atlantic operations, flying a schedule of approximately 12 flights each month between New York and Frankfurt.

The Rättviks Spelmanslag group, leaving New York for Stockholm on a Flying Tiger Line C-54, July 3, 1956. Aviation News Pictures

High-road for 68 homeward bound Scots. More than 4,000 people turned out at Niagara Falls, New York, to bid a bonnie farewell to Flying Tiger Line Douglas C-54B N30058 which took the Clan Mackenzie to Edinburgh, Scotland. Clyde R. Telaak

Photos Clyde R. Telaak

ICEM charter flight. An Intergovernmental Committee for European Migrants charter flight operated by Flying Tiger Line Douglas C-54B N30058 arrives in New York Idlewild from Munich, deplaning its passengers, shown here heading for the customs area. These flights operated on a year-round contract basis with the ICEM group, which supervised the migration of European displaced persons to the United States under sponsorship of racial and religious groups such as the American Fund for Czech Refugees, the Catholic Committee for Refugees, the Tolstoy Foundation, the National Lutheran Council, the Hebrew Immigration Aid Society, and the Church World Service. Aviation News Pictures

A Flying Tiger crew boarding a DC-6 MATS flight at New York, bound to Burtonwood air base, England, and Frankfurt, Germany. The crew on the steps, left to right, are William Towner, co-pilot; Ricky Bryant, ground hostess, Navigator Emory Warner, stewardesses Mary Zeigler, Carol Hetfield and Mary Ann Cooke, Captain Ray Allen and First Officer John Salamon. Aviation News Pictures

Historic first Tiger flight with Hungarian refugees. To the long list of flight accomplishments which the Flying Tiger Line amassed in its first 11 years of operation, possibly the most historic of all took place on November 21, 1956. 62 Hungarian refugees arrived at McGuire Air Force Base, New Jersey on a Flying Tiger Line Douglas C-54B N88940 after a 39 hour flight from Vienna, Austria. After disembarkation, they lined up to listen to a welcome address from Army Secretary Wilber Marion Brucker, lower right, bareheaded, as he spoke through an interpreter. The refugees were then bussed by the Army to adjoining Camp Kilmer, renamed Camp Mercy where they completed the immigration processing two days later before going to new homes. The crew members for the inaugural flight were Captains Frank Hawkins and Bus Loane, First Officer Ralph Mitchell, Co-Pilot David Vachon, Navigators Robert Lowe and Jack Craig, and stewardesses Virginia Earle and Rosemarie Inderbitzen. United Press International

Flying Tigers' first Lockheed Super Constellation. From left, Vice-President George T. Cussen of FTL, Vice President Carl Squier, one of the founders of Lockheed Aircraft Corp., Vice-President Bill Bartling and Vice-President Frank Lynott, both of FTL, moving the final barrel section of the first fuselage in to place.

December 1956, District Sales Manager Bernard Tenney (left) and Miss Flying Tiger, Maxine Davidson (centre) pulling the first Flying Tiger Line Super Constellation fuselage out of Lockheed's pressure dock to the final assembly area for the addition of wings, tail and engines. The first Flying Tiger's L-1049H was N6911C, fleet number 801.

The first Flying Tigers L-1049H N6911C (serial 4804) was delivered at Burbank on February 1, 1957. It crashed on approach to Adak Naval Air Facility, in the Aleutian Islands on March 15, 1962 killing Flight Engineer J.M. Johnstone.

Watson Photos

Bob Prescott is sharing the December 1956 edition of Tigereview with a group of four Hungarian refugees who fought as freedom fighters in Budapest in the October 1956 revolution and then escaped the Soviets and local secret police after they ran out of ammunition. A group of 57 men and women brought to Los Angeles under sponsorship of the Los Angeles Presbytery came to the attention of Robert Prescott, who referred them to Flying Tigers' Personnel Department. Since they were skilled mechanics, they quickly qualified for work in the airline's Burbank shops. Left to right are Joseph Varga, 23, former aviation instrument assembly worker, Anthony Kovacs, 28, formerly an airplane engine mechanic, Bob Prescott, Leslie Varga, 21, brother of Joe, also an aviation instrument man and Anthony Zandor, 38, cousin of Anthony Kovacs, a 5,800-hour pilot formerly with the Hungarian Lufthansa.

Bill R. Watson.

L-1049H N6913C in March 1957 on the final assembly line at the Lockheed plant at Burbank, California, where the finishing touches are applied to Flying Tiger's Super Constellation fleet. N6912C is in front, almost ready to roll out from the assembly hall.

Inauguration ceremony for the new Super H cargo service by the Flying Tiger Line at Burbank. On May 4, 1957, Robert Prescott chaired the ceremonies marking the inauguration of new Super H cargo service. On the podium, from left to right, Robert Prescott, Joann Waddell, unknown, and Helen Ruth Prescott. The first Tiger Constellation flew out of Burbank on the night of May 11 carrying 42,800 pounds, said to be the largest commercial air cargo load ever flown from Burbank at that time.

On display at the May 4, 1957 inaugural ceremonies were 43,000 pounds of flower boxes, representing the weight which the Constellation can carry. From left, models Joann Waddel, Geri Mirman and Sandy McLean wave on the Transocean Air Lines steps next to the newly delivered Super H Constellation N6915C.

Low-cost air travel meets the peak of passenger comfort with the inauguration by the Flying Tiger Line of Super Constellation flights. This shot shows how passengers in 1957 on the Super H, which seated either 96 or 114, ride in perfect comfort. Three stewardesses took care of passenger needs and served hot meals aloft.

On June 21, 1957, Flying Tiger Line Douglas DC-6A N34953 made a forced landing, following loss of power on all engines, on a sandbar in Jamaica Bay, two miles southwest of its take off from New York Idlewild Airport, on a ferry flight to Dover, Delaware, before a trip to Chateauroux, France, via Gander, Newfoundland, to pick up Army personnel. The flight crew consisted of Captain Gregory P. Thomas, Co-pilot William H. Seamans and Flight Engineer Bernard P. Palamar. Six passengers, all deadheading employees were Robert Dayton, navigator; Stewardesses Jeannine Cussen, Eugenia Johnson and Berangere Reubens; Howard F. Amrhein, first officer; and Guy G. McAlister, flight engineer. The three flight crew members were uninjured but three of the six employee-passengers – Dayton, Amrhein, and Miss Cussen – incurred minor injuries. The aircraft couldn't get above 100 feet after leaving runway 31 and made a wheels-up landing, receiving substantial damage and salt water immersion. The cause of the accident was contaminated ADI (antidetonant injection) fluid in the engines. The ADI tanks of the aircraft had been filled with ethylene glycol instead of methanol-water by mistake. The aircraft was later repaired. After a long career, it was last seen in 2012 in New Mexico at Santa Teresa Dona Ana County airport as N620NA painted in American Airlines colours for an advertisement. U.S. Navy

General Chennault and his pilots. In June 1957, the AVG Flying Tigers relive their exploits at the Southern California mountain resort of Ojai Valley. Together in Chennault's cottage during a business meeting, from left to right, are Joe Poshefko, with cigarette; Ernest "Red" Holmes, with hand on chin; Ed Rector in chair; Arvid Olson, in front of Ed; Freemen Ricketts, in white t-shirt; Joe Rosbert, behind Ricketts, Claire Chennault; Dick Rossi; Robert Prescott and Tommy Haywood. Chennault was the creator and leader of the American Volunteer Group of pilots and mechanics serving in China, better known as the Flying Tigers. He died on July 27, 1958.

Watson Photos

In Ojai valley, 38 miles north of Los Angeles, Dick Rossi, president of Flying Tigers group, moves in camera for a close-up shot of actress Jane Mansfield at the reunion of Flying Tigers in late June 1957 that gathered a band of 87 pilots and 165 ground personnel around General Claire Lee Chennault. During the events, Miss Mansfield and Chennault presented the Flying Tiger Pilot award to Alvin M. 'Tex' Johnston. The award, given to express the fliers' admiration to those now leading the way in aviation, was bestowed on Johnston for his work as chief test pilot on the Boeing 707. AVG Flying Tigers Association

The Big Reach. The Flying Tiger Line inaugurated its Big Reach All-Constellation airfreight service in October 1957 with overnight transcontinental delivery to most of the airline's terminals. Several officials, shippers, public and press conference events were organised to spark the imagination of the shipping public over the new air freight service. This included multiple winners of Miss California Industry at Burbank for Flying Tigers' first Super H non-stop cargo flight to New York. Left to right are Billie J. Hallam, Miss Los Angeles Industry; Pat Reed, Miss Calavo; Moni Blowers, Miss Sunkist and Judy Whitcher, Miss San Fernando Valley Industry.

Watson Photos

Captain Malcolm E. "Mac" Canaday holding a Three-and-a-half foot King Crab which he flew from Kodiak, Alaska into Detroit on a Super H flight was chosen as the key picture for a striking Detroit Free Press picture-story layout in November 1957. It was blown up to nearly full-page size. Nine other pictures were used in the big spread, showing orchids, elephants, horses, dogs, monkeys, strawberries, aircraft loading scenes, and even an Army mechanical "mule". The Flying Tiger Line public relations department later distributed more than 1,000 copies of the special supplement to leading shippers.

Sixteen Charlie. As a result of labour shortages in the industrial areas of Great Britain, 114 Jamaicans left Kingston by BOAC charter flight for London in the late evening of March 29, 1958 to seek jobs in Britain. Flying Tiger Line Super H N6916C was first positioned from Idlewild to Jamaica with a double crew. Six hours later she was on the ground at Palisadoes Airport in Kingston. The flight departed in the late evening of March 29 with its load of emigrants to Montego Bay on the other side of the island where a full load of fuel was taken on for the nine-hour flight to Gander. After passengers were served a breakfast in the airport restaurant and Sixteen Charlie refueled, the aircraft reached London on March 31 in the morning, taking seven hours and fifteen minutes to cross the Atlantic. The aircraft was operated by the company's eastern contracts division and fitted in between the ceaseless freight service, and were an important part of the company's programme for maintaining the maximum utilisation of their aircraft. Some of the pictures were used in articles published by Shell Aviation News in September and November 1958.   Lambert

"Fasten seat belts, please... We're off."

Lambert

Flying Tigress Club. In the mid 1950s, a group of women whose common bond was their husbands' career in aviation got together to know each other better. They formed the Flying Tigress Club. Any wife whose husband was Flying Tigers flight crew was eligible for membership - pilot, navigator, flight engineer. Organized first as a social effort, the club, through family experiences, took on a greater goal, helping those in need and donating money to deserving individuals, charities, societies, Scout organisations, Red Cross and many more. In this January 1958 picture, they enjoyed memories of many meetings at the club. Seated, left to right, are: Mrs Tom Haywood, secretary; Mrs Jack Salomon, vice president; Mrs Jack Reichl, treasurer; and Mrs Bob Conrath. Standing, left to right: Mrs Egner Gunderson, Mrs John deKramer, Mrs Bob Martin and Mrs Pete Baxter. Three other board members, President Ann Wall, Mrs Jack Martin and Mrs Dick Stuelke, were absent when the picture was made.

Silky Sullivan, a famous thoroughbred racehorse best known for its come-from-behind racing style, moved unconcernedly onto a Flying Tiger Line Douglas DC-6A N34953 at the San Francisco terminal on the evening of Sunday, April 13, 1958 for a flight to Louisville with five other horses for the Kentucky Derby. On the horse ramp leading into the aircraft, a banner had been affixed. It read: "Good Luck to Silky Sullivan. The Flying Horse with a Flying Finish. The Flying Tigers."

One hundred and fourteen members of The Pastorius Association of Greater New York, a German-American society, departed New York International Airport in July 1958 aboard a Super H for a pilgrimage flight to Frankfurt. Among the passengers were members and families of the German-American organisation en route to the town of Sommershausen, Germany, to commemorate the birth anniversary of Franz Daniel Pastorius who settled with a group of weavers in Germantown, Pennsylvania in 1683. The pilgrimage group of men, women and children made a formal presentation of a commemorative plaque to the town of Sommershausen and also toured Germany participating in songfests and visiting points of historical interest. Aviation News Pictures

Tiger Dick Rossi with Tiger Girl Shirley Haven in front of a Curtiss P-40 during the 1958 Flying Tigers American Volunteer Group (AVG) and China National Aviation Corporation (CNAC) joint reunion in San Francisco. *The 6 Watson Bros.*

In August 1958, Mary Lynn, assistant chief stewardess at San Francisco, was among 50 airline stewardesses whose role in aviation was featured in the August 25 issue of Life Magazine. Miss Lynn spent a week in New York in May 1958 along with stewardesses of more than fifty airlines being photographed for the Life story. Afterward, she was one of seven stewardesses asked by Life to stay over for an additional three days for more pictures to depict typical scenes in the lives of stewardesses. In arranging the picture, Life editors said that the picture marked the first time that stewardess representatives from all of America's airlines had been brought together for a group shot. Mary Lynn served on Flying Tiger overseas aircraft since May 1957, when she joined the company and began flying the North Atlantic. Later, she became a check stewardess on the Pacific and was promoted assistant chief stewardess in summer 1958.   Watson Photo

Industrial and civic leaders of Southern California trade and manufacturing areas gathered at Flying Tiger's Burbank base as a sixth Super H Constellation was placed in service on Flying Tiger's domestic air freight system in mid-October 1958, resulting in widespread schedule improvements. Left: In contrast to the eight-hour non-stop schedule of the Super H from Los Angeles to New York, carrying more than 40,000 pounds of freight, it took a covered wagon about 100 days to haul 2,000 pounds of freight about half as far a century ago, from Missouri to California. John Higgins, Flying Tiger Line vice president, and Chancellor Raymond B. Allen of the University of California at Los Angeles, chairman of the Los Angeles Chamber of Commerce Air Transportation Committee are holding a flower box with Miss California of 1958, Sandra Jennings, on the covered wagon in front of Super H N6923C delivered a few months earlier. Right: With a CEC electronic detector are left to right, John Price, Chamber of Commerce president; R. W. Winegar, traffic manager of Bendix Pacific Division; Miss California; and Lew Ayres, Flying Tigers sales. Watson Photos

High density Super H. Flying Tiger Line L-1049H "high density" passenger version with 106 seats.

One of the last of Flying Tiger Curtiss C-46 fleet ship No. 989 is ready for sale at Burbank in December 1958 to Aero Carga of Mexico. Still wearing the Flying Tiger red-white-blue striping and titled California, N67989 went first into an extensive three-week full interior modification to convert the C-46F into a 44-seater aircraft. The aircraft later became XA-MOJ, registration already visible on the wings.

Another chapter in the saga of a one-man baby-lift which brought 1,176 unwanted children to homes in America was concluded on Christmas weekend 1958 when a Flying Tiger Super H Constellation landed in Portland, Oregon on December 27 with 107 Korean children. They were accompanied by 18 nurses, doctors and stewardesses and the flight thus transported probably the largest number of persons carried on a single aircraft across the Pacific up until then: 125. The baby lift was in a continuing series started in 1956 by Harry Holt, a Creswell, Oregon, farmer, in an effort to find homes for abandoned or orphaned Korean children. The project reached the point where Holt established an adoption agency at Seoul, Korea. When the Super H landed at Portland, more than 100 waiting parents from 21 states were on hand to meet their new children. Left: Still sporting their winter caps with ear flaps, as it had been snowing when they left Seoul on December 26, two older boys bid goodbye and get a present of a ball from Stewardess Anna Lou Spino. Right: These children with Stewardess Susan Carll didn't get a kick out of the wet weather which greeted them at the end of their trip in Portland.

Photos Mather

Flying Tiger crewmen bid adieu to one of the nurses on the Pacific baby lift and her tiny charge. Left to right are: Navigator Sy Cohen, Captain Al Perrault, Co-pilot R. J. Raines, Flight Engineer Leroy C. Tripp. *Mather*

The first Rolls-Royce engine for installation on a Boeing 707 passenger jet for British Overseas Airways Corp. was flown by the Flying Tiger Line in December 1958. First engine to enter the country under the Custom Entry Bond Bill H. R. 9923 passed by the US Congress in 1958 to permit temporary free importation under bond for exportation, the shipment originated at London airport, being flown to New York by Seaboard & Western Airlines; thence by Flying Tigers to Seattle on a Super H.

Crew room in Kingston, Jamaica with Lawrence F. "Dad" Luccio between a stewardess and a pilot in 1959. Larry was a pilot during World War II, and afterward operated a flying school before becoming a pilot for the Flying Tiger Line in 1950. He quickly picked up his nickname because of his generous nature and his willingness to take care of everyone he flew with, almost like a father.

Hugh Harvey

Flying Tiger Line Lockheed L-1049H N6912C loading at Burbank in January 1959.

Burbank February 1959. Flying Tiger Line Lockheed L-1049H N6915C being prepared for flight at the Burbank Lockheed Air Terminal in 1959. With a fuel stick in his right hand, the flight engineer on the wing is going to check the quantity in one of the tip tanks. This was done to compare with the fuel gauges in the cockpit and to ensure the fuel load. The tip tank gauges were unreliable and fuel amounts were questionable at times.

February 1959, two Flying Tiger Line Lockheed L-1049Hs being loaded and serviced at Burbank.

February 1959, a Tiger Lockheed L-1049H taxiing towards the active runway at Burbank. In the background on the left are Eastern and Braniff L-188s being made ready for delivery by Lockheed.

L-1049H N6913C fleet number 803 was delivered to the Flying Tiger Line in March 1957. The aircraft crashed into a residential and industrial area in the San Fernando Valley one and a quarter miles west of Burbank Airport at 22.12 hrs (PST) on December 14, 1962, killing all on board and three local residents on the ground. Captain Karl C. Rader, First Officer David L. Crapo, and Flight Engineer Jack W. Grey assumed flight crew duties on the flight. Two non-revenue passengers also boarded at Chicago, John A. Olson, husband of Flying Tigers employee Janet Olson and Mrs. Violet Blazek, Flying Tigers field administrator. The aircraft was on a scheduled domestic cargo service en route from Chicago to Burbank, and was destroyed by fire and impact. The airport was shrouded in fog and the crew were making an ILS approach to runway 07. Position was acknowledged 2 miles from the runway end and 20 seconds before the crash. The probable cause of the accident was the incapacitation of the captain who had severe coronary artery disease during a critical situation, resulting in loss of control, from which the co-pilot was unable to recover. Compounding the severity of the situation, it is likely that the captain fell forward onto the controls, limiting aft movement of the control column to the extent that the aircraft could not be rapidly rotated to a positive climb attitude. Further, because of a low fog bank condition with the relatively good visibility above, it is believed that the co-pilot Crapo would not be monitoring the captain's approach as closely as he would in an IFR situation. Therefore, following the rapid deviation from glide slope it is probable that N6913C entered the fog bank before Crapo could fully assume control of the aircraft and then transition to instrument flight conditions.

Jan Boon Collection

Typical turkey-egg on-loading scene shows Jerry Fredine, cargo handler, easing egg cartons aboard N6912C, a Super H, in February 1959 while Cargo Supervisor Bill White keeps the conveyor filled. Assistant General Sales Manager George Zettler was working in Flying Tigers' San Francisco station when he originally set up the business of moving turkey eggs from California and Oregon ranches to farms in Iowa, Minnesota, Wisconsin, Indiana, Ohio, Michigan and on to eastern seaboard states such as Pennsylvania and New York. By 1958, 500 tons of turkey eggs were shipped annually by the Flying Tiger Line.

Up and close with the new Douglas DC-8. Robert Prescott at the controls of the Douglas DC-8 prototype during an evaluation flight out of Long Beach, California, where the new jet was built. Accompanied by Vice Presidents Frank Lynott and Bill Bartling, Prescott made a thorough inspection of the aircraft as part of an intensive study under way by Flying Tigers management to select the best type of jet aircraft for future operations. Besides the DC-8, Prescott, Lynott and Bartling studied jet cargo proposals from Boeing, Lockheed and Convair. At the time, Prescott and his team were assessing whether prop jet aircraft such as the Lockheed Electra, or pure jet, such as the DC-8, would be most efficient on Flying Tiger freight routes. Irrespective of which type was finally selected, Prescott said his experience flying the DC-8 was "one of the greatest in my life."

Ground personnel on the steps of Super H N6918C after interior cleaning at Burbank in March 1959.

173

Busy Flying Tiger ramp scene in Burbank around March 1959 with Super H N6916C being hand-loaded through both forward and rear cargo doors.

Silver Spoon, a thoroughbred racehorse, boarding Flying Tiger Super H N6925C at Burbank on April 12, 1959 on a non-stop charter flight of six hours, 15 minutes to Churchill Downs, Louisville, Kentucky. The crew on that day was Captain Thor Garton, Co-Pilot Bob Wish, and Flight Engineer William George.

Flying Tiger's Burbank hangars were the scene of a press and TV breakfast on April 15, 1959 which reunited three men who flew together in China during the historic days of the original Flying Tigers. Pictured here, left to right, are Robert Prescott, Colonel Gregory "Pappy" Boyington, USMC Ret.; and Captain Dick Rossi, president of the American Volunteer Group Flying Tigers Association (AVGFTA). The occasion was Boyington's departure on a 9,000 mile 45 day tour of 30 American cities to fill speaking and press engagements in connection with his best-seller book, Baa Baa Black Sheep, and sale of movie rights to Columbia Studios for $250,000. It is the story of his fabulous career from his days in the Flying Tigers to the completion of his Marine Corps career, during which he became the top "ace" of World War II.   AVG Flying Tigers Association

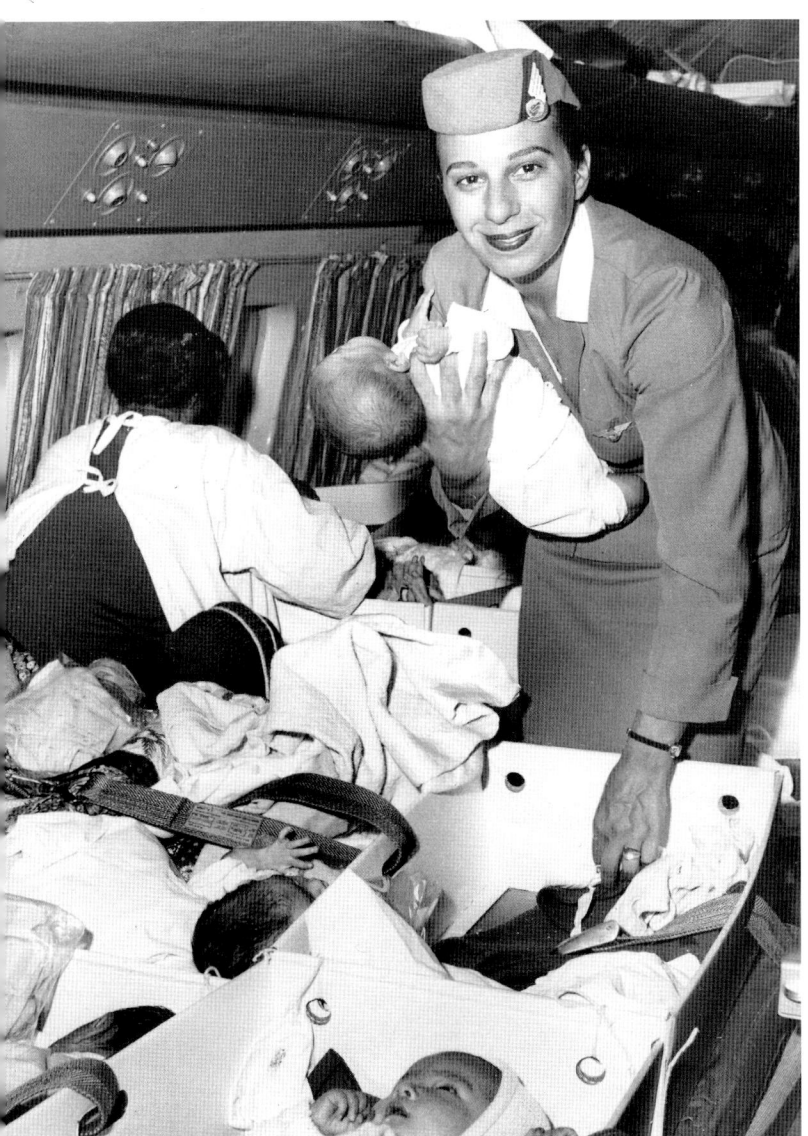 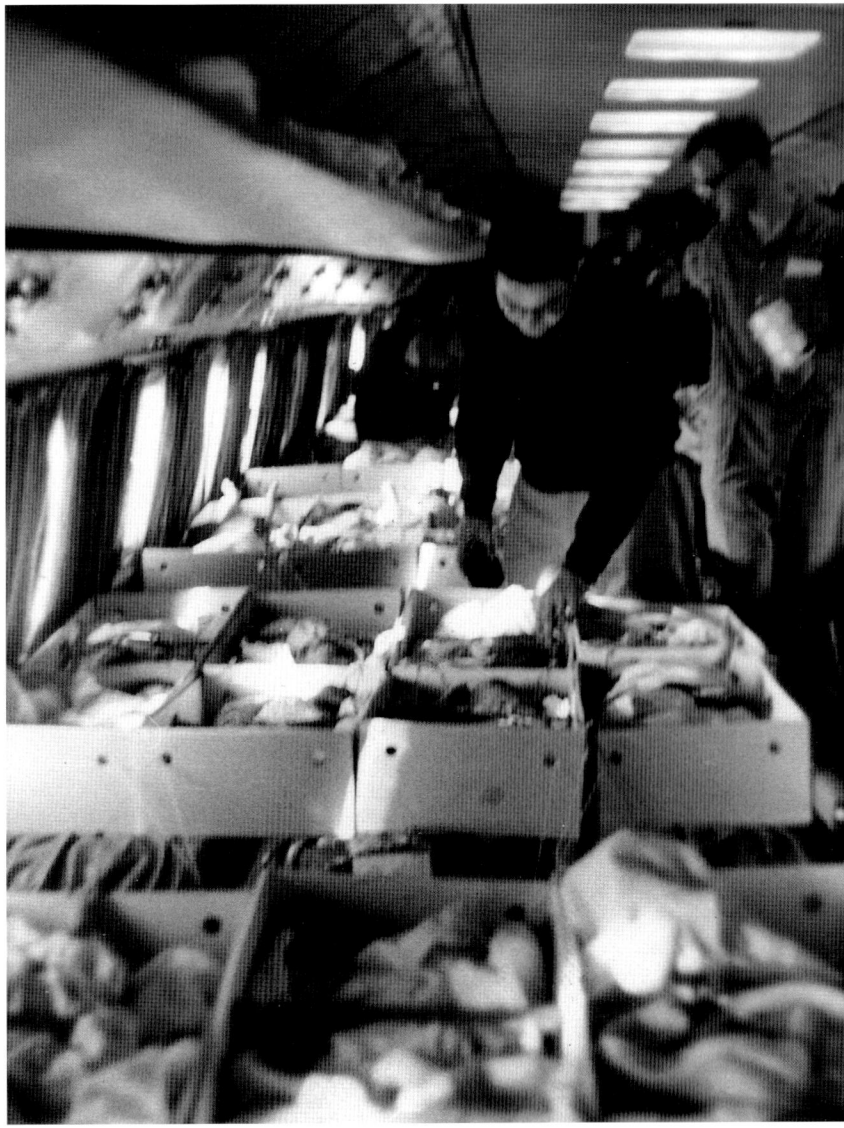

Another Flying Tiger Baby Lift with 112 Korean orphans from Seoul to Portland, successfully completed in April 1959. Flying Tiger Stewardess Treso Koken and some of her charges on the flight. Babies were flown in cradles fitted across the Super H cabin.

First jet air freighter. A $55,000,000 order for a fleet of 10 turbine-powered freighters was announced on May 14, 1959 by Robert Prescott. The contract had been signed with Canadair Limited, a Montreal-based subsidiary of General Dynamics Corporation, for the early 1961 delivery of the CL-44D-4, with a swing-tail loading design. Pictured here is a scale model of the Canadair CL-44 featuring Bristol Britannia cockpit windows and an experimental Flying Tiger Line livery concept where the cheatline ended around a large T tail logo. Originally named Pacemaker, neither name nor livery were adopted, though the dotted cheatline was retained.

CL-44.com Collection

The 1959 Flying Tigers and CNAC joint reunion. Gathered at the Southern California mountain resort of Ojai in July 1959 with their families and friends for their fifth reunion, and first since the death in 1958 of the Tigers' famed commander, Lt. Gen. Claire Lee Chennault. Robert Prescott (left) and Dick Rossi carry flame-haired actress and singer Rhonda Fleming from the Bell 47J Ranger of the Northrop Corporation on her arrival at the reunion.

The two-story headquarters of the Flying Tiger Line in Burbank at 10811 Sherman Way in August 1958.

Flying Tiger Line

Flying Tiger Super H N6912C on final approach around 1959.

Jacques Guillem Collection

Flying Tiger Super H N6915C at Chicago, around 1959. On December 24, 1964, the aircraft crashed into Sweeneys Ridge, 4.3 miles west-southwest of San Francisco airport. Much of the wreckage was consumed in the intense ground fire which followed. The three crewmembers, Captain Jabez Albert Richard, First Officer Daniel White Hennessy and Flight Engineer Paul M. Entz, were killed. There were no passengers. Flight 282 was scheduled as a domestic cargo flight from San Francisco to New York. The CAB determined that the probable cause of this accident was that the pilot, for undetermined reasons, deviated from departure course into an area of rising terrain where downdraft activity and turbulence affected the climb capability of the aircraft sufficiently to prevent terrain clearance.

On October 3, 1959, Flying Tiger Line personnel in Burbank handled the difficult job of loading the Aston Martin race car which Stirling Moss of England drove in the Times-Mirror Grand Prix at Riverside on October 10-11 aboard Super H N6925C.

Arriving at Burbank in December 1959 on a Super H is Sita, a 700-pound, 18-month-old baby elephant from India. From left to right; Robert Prescott, Mayor Poulson, Art Linkletter and Peter Prescott, son of Robert Prescott and Helen Ruth. The 6 Watson Bros.

Robert Prescott was well aware of the hold Hollywood had on the American public and he developed ties with the Hollywood elite, as demonstrated by the many beautiful movie actresses and actors he was photographed with. The photo of Prescott feeding milk to Jayne Mansfield's son Mickey Hargitay Jr. was taken around 1960. A sex symbol while under contract at 20th Century Fox, Mansfield was known for her well-publicised personal life and publicity stunts. In her short life, she had several box office successes and won a Theatre World Award and a Golden Globe Award.   The 6 Watson Bros. Photography, Inc.

Flying Tiger Super H N6921C under a rainbow in Guam circa 1960. The aircraft was lost on March 15, 1962 when operating a MATS cargo flight from Travis AFB in California to Saigon, with four refuelling stops - Honolulu, Wake Island, Guam and Clark AFB in the Philippines. It departed Travis on March 14 with 96 military passengers aboard, mainly electronics and communications specialists. Also on board were three members of the Vietnamese military and a multiple crew of 11 under the command of Captain Gregory P. Thomas. After departing from Guam on March 15 for an estimated time en route of six hours and 19 minutes, the crew reported its position, cruising at 18,000 feet above the clouds. This was the last radio transmission received from N6921C. The subsequent search, one of the most extensive ever conducted in aviation history at that time, covered 144,000 square miles and utilized 1,300 people, 48 aircraft, and eight surface vessels. A total of 377 air sorties were flown which involved over 3,417 flying hours. Despite the thoroughness of the search, nothing was found which could conceivably be linked to the missing aircraft or its occupants. Due to the lack of any substantiating evidence the Civil Aeronautics Board (CAB) was unable to state with any degree of certainty the exact fate of N6921C. Other crew members were First Officer Robert J. Wish, Second Officer Robbie J. Gayzaway, Flight Engineer George M. Nau, Flight Engineer Clayton E. McClellan, Navigator William T. Kennedy, Navigator Grady R. Burt, Jr., and Stewardesses Patricia Wassum, Hildegarde Muller, Barbara Wamsley, and Christel Reiter.

In early April 1960, when Kenneth Allen of the Burroughs Corporation got word he was to be transferred from Dayton to Los Angeles, he naturally decided to fly. His British car, a Morris Minor, flew, too. It was loaded aboard a Flying Tiger Line Super H at Detroit, destination Los Angeles, and got to California just about the time Allen did.

Movie star aids Community Chest campaign. Actress Jayne Mansfield, Miss Flying Tiger of 1958, gets a full hearing on the Chest campaign from Bob Levy (centre) and Paul Robert of Maintenance in the Burbank hangar. The 6 Watson Bros.

Photo shoot with Jayne Mansfield and Robert Prescott passing out pledge cards to the Burbank employees, John Stowell, "Rod" Rodriguez, Manny Bernal, Frank Simpkins, John Kuncewitch, Harley Chambers and Tony Kovacs. Flying Tiger participation in the 1960 Community Chest campaign raised contributions to support development projects in the San Fernando Valley.   The 6 Watson Bros.

A happy group of 98 American Youth Hostels students gaily wave farewell as they prepare to board a Flying Tiger Line Super H Constellation for Europe in July 1960 after being stranded in New York for four days. Justine Cline, AYH director, had high praise for Flying Tigers' ability to perform the rescue flight within 24 hours, and the cooperation of Jim Correa and Kurt Jordon, veteran Flying Tigers employees who handled the flight's departure. Aviation News Pictures

A group of children from the San Fernando Valley Troop Three of Girl Scouts exploring a Flying Tigers Super H Constellation freighter at Burbank in March 1961. Organized by the Personnel Department, Burbank maintenance and freight station facilities tours were very popular as Flying Tigers understood the importance of advertising the nation's only certified transcontinental all-cargo airline to future generations.

Airfreight specialist. In 1960, the Flying Tiger Line ran a creative campaign in mainstream newspapers with six advertisements promoting non-stop overnight service, teletyped advance manifest system, expedited door-to-door delivery, personalised customer service, lowest rates and for being the only transcontinental all-cargo airline. Reproduced here are two of the series of advertisements which significantly drove sales at the time.

First of ten Tiger CL 44's. Flying Tiger Canadair CL-44D4-2 temporarily registered CF-NND-X next to a RCAF CL-44-6/CC-106 Yukon at Canadair's Cartierville plant in May 1961. The aircraft first flew on May 10, 1961 being temporarily registered to Canadair Ltd. Delivered to the Flying Tiger Line as N451T on Jun 1, 1960, it was sold to Loftleidir on April 30, 1968 as TF-LLJ, named Thorvaldur Eiriksson before going to Cargolux on January 4, 1970, named City of Luxembourg. Leased to Young Cargo on March 4, 1975 and registered OO-ELJ and named Spirit of Charleroi, it returned to Cargolux on August 14, 1975 to be immediately sold to Affretair on August 25, 1975 as TR-LVO. Transferred to Air Gabon Cargo on May 10, 1980, it was leased to Royal Air Maroc between December 1980 and February 1981. Seriously damaged by fire whilst undergoing maintenance at Salisbury, Zimbabwe on February 5, 1982, the first Tiger CL-44 was damaged beyond repair and broken up.

Two Flying Tigers CL-44D4-2s are made ready at Canadair's Cartierville plant in May 1961 with CF-NND-X (fleet number 306 and future N451T) in the foreground, tail swung open; and behind, N450T still wearing its test registration CF-NBP-X. In the background between factory building are a Canadair CC-106 Yukon of the Canadian Armed Forces and another Tiger CL-44, N452T, tail opened.

Use of automatic loading equipment for the CL-44 is demonstrated at the Canadair factory in Cartierville Airport, where the ships were built. The huge scissor lift handles single loads as heavy as 20,000 pounds. *CL-44.com Collection*

Air-to-air view of N451T during a test flight and photo shoot. Tigers' first turbine-powered airfreighter, the CL-44 had a cruising speed of 375 miles per hour over a range of 3,000 miles. Its unique swing-tail design permitted straight-in loading of its 65,000 pound payload much faster than its piston-powered predecessors. *CL-44.com Collection*

First of ten Tiger CL-44s cheered on arrival at Burbank. "There she is!" This simple but dramatic exclamation from someone in a crowd of several hundred Flying Tiger employees and visitors at the airline's Burbank base compressed into three crisp words which years of planning, sweat and toil had now delivered. The date was June 2, 1961. With Captain Arthur Seymour, Director of Flight Training, Executive Vice President-Operations Frank Lynott, and Captain Oakley Smith, Eastern Region Chief Pilot, at the controls, the big ship, almost slowly it seemed, skimmed the deck at 200 on a pass across the field with barely a whisper from its engines, before landing and taxiing in front of a large crowd at Burbank.

June 2, 1961 marked the arrival of Flying Tigers' first Canadair CL-44 at Burbank and the entry of the airline into the jet age with history's first swing-tail, turbine-powered airfreighter. N451T, fleet number 306, the first of the ten Tiger CL-44s, first arrived in New York Idlewild on June 1 for a complex customs stop and to meet a delegation headed by Executive Vice President Fred Benninger and General Counsel Norman Meyers to see Executive Vice President Frank Lynott accompany the ship in from Montreal.

Conley

Flying Tigers Board Chairman Samuel B. Mosher and President Robert Prescott with a cake baked especially for the occasion by Chefs Orchid Airline Caterers at Idlewild Airport, New York, and sent to Burbank aboard the CL-44.

Robert Prescott beside one of the Rolls-Royce engines and directly behind him, the CL-44's swing tail open and at right angles to the fuselage, an aircraft view never before seen at Burbank.

Robert Prescott and Paul Kelly, who flew Flying Tigers' famous first grape flight in 1945 do a little reminiscing.

Robert Prescott with flight crew, left to right, Vice President Frank Lynott, Prescott, Captain Arthur F. Seymour, Bud Scouten, Canadair Chief Production Pilot, Chief Flight Engineer John Ristaino and Superintendent Don Fry. Captain Oakley Smith, also aboard, was lost in the crowd when this picture was made.

The crew of brand-new CL-44 N451T at the Burbank terminal on July 16, 1961 en route to Travis Air For Base, near San Francisco, for its inaugural MATS flight under the command of Captain Cliff Groh. From left to right, Flight Engineer Ted Menk, Flight Engineer Al Mobley, Navigator Ernie Hickman, Captain Don Sanders, Captain Ralph Hedden and Cliff Groh. From Travis, 51T carried a near-record load of 150 people, 134 passengers and a crew and inspection team of 16.
The 6th Watson Bros. Photography Inc.

Officialdom views Flying Tigers CL-44 in capitol debut. In Washington, at a press conference on August 28-29, 1961 during the first public display of the new CL-44, left to right, J. Geoffrey Notman, president, Canadair; Robert Prescott; Norman L. Meyers, Flying Tiger Line General Councel; Wally Longstreth, Editor, Air Cargo Magazine; and Marshall Meyers. Getting the aircraft to Washington was a major project because the event came in the midst of Tiger programs for crew training, modification of aircraft for both freight and passenger operation and contract demands of the military for use on the Pacific.

Two unusual visitors to the CL-44 cockpit in Washington on August 28-29, 1961 during the first public display of the new CL-44 are Sister Charles Gabriel in the captain's seat and Sister Mary Lucy.

Crew of the CL-44 during the first public display in Washington on August 28-29, 1961, left to right, Dena Millard, Captain Oakley Smith, Jean Manning, Captain Ernest "Bus" Loane, Pat Siemens, Flight Engineer Gene Olsen, Myrna Lee Scott. Kneeling in foreground are (left) Doc Powell, and Joe Healy, operating the swingtail mechanism and announcing system.

On the steps of N447T, during the first public display of the new CL-44 in Washington, left to right, George Oberdorf; Congressman Victor Wickersham of Oklahoma, holding the Swingtail-44 brochure, and Miss French Prescott, daughter of Bob Prescott.

Graphic view of the Allen Loader carried by the CL-44 to Washington, inserting a freight pallet into N447T during the public display.
CL-44.com Collection

Briefing in Honolulu around September 1961 shows this transpacific Super H crew on the Tigers MATS contract operation getting a few last minute details settled. Left to right are First Officer Dick Petrick, Augie Droll of Maintenance, Flight Engineer Ted Menk, Station Agent Steve Berger, Captain Ray Allen, and Navigator Bill Arlicky.

While Foreman Wallace Stevens (left foreground) conducts a check of a huge De Havilland propeller used on the new CL-44, Flying Tiger and De Havilland officials check results. Left to right are James McLachlan, Flying Tigers' director of maintenance and engineering; D. S. Hyde, De Havilland Manager of Service from Hatfield, England; Norman Battey, FTL De Havilland representative; and Superintendent Joe Baker of Flying Tiger Shops and Facilities. CL-44.com Collection

In the cockpit of a Tiger CL-44, on the left seat, is John R. "Dobbie" Dobson, senior Flying Tiger Line captain hired in April 1949, starting engine number four for a test flight.

The captain's instrument panel of the Canadair CL-44 N447T.

The 6 Watson Bros.

44 sets records. By December 1961, the swingtail CL-44, in operation on Flying Tigers' overseas routes, had established impressive lift records. On its first transpacific freight flight, it carried a record 61,000 pounds of freight to Tokyo, while another ship airlifted 157 people. But when Ground Operations got two complete Lockheed F-104G supersonic tactical aircraft inside the 44's hold, even cargo handlers who'd seen it all tipped their caps. Complete with engines, two tail units and two sets of wings, the F-104s were loaded in the 44 to prove that this method of transportation offered rapid and economical deployment of such aircraft to NATO nations to meet urgent delivery schedules. Following the initial trial loading at the Montreal plant of Canadair, the Flying Tiger Line began the actual transportation of F-104s, loading the aircraft at its Burbank base and transporting them to Germany and Netherlands.

CL-44.com Collection

Just a little something to go to work in, or at least that is what Ginger Ford of Burbank Sales was dreaming, according to the photographer, when he lined up this shot in late 1961 of a $21,000 hand-built Ferrari racer brought in from New York by the Tigers for a west coast race. Of course, it took five men to get it started with a good push. On hand to help are, left to right, Larry Bakken, Ed Trott, Ginger Ford, Bill Henry, Jess Coulter and Steve Baird. The 6 Watson Bros. Photography Inc.

Curtiss C-46F N67985 came to the Tigers in August 1950 and flew all over North America for more than 12 years before being sold to Pacific International Airways in late December 1961. Saying goodbye was a sad moment for, left to right, Tom Haywood, Joe Baker, Buck Buchanan, Al Penrose, Karl Rader, John Dewey and John Murray. This machine was last of fleet of 32.   Phil Glickman

Super H Constellation N6911C was heavily damaged at Grand Island, Nebraska, on December 1, 1961. The incident occurred after she landed for refuelling. With a full load of cargo and fuel, she was taxiing out for take off when a section of the ramp gave way. The right main landing gear went into the hole, damaging the gear, two propellers on the right side, the right wing and the tail section. After two months of extensive repairs by an eight-man maintenance crew headed by Willie Skaggs from Burbank, Captains Art Seymour and Jack Martin ferried the aircraft on February 7, 1962, for a final checkout at Burbank before re-entering service on February 10.

Tigers in Hong Kong. What used to be one of Tigers' most difficult pioneering air freight projects, the loading, airlift, and offloading of long, heavy ship drive shafts, soon became a routine operation. The line's growing reputation as specialists in this field led to a contract which saw a 24 foot, 34,618 pound drive shaft airlifted from Newark to Hong Kong aboard N6912C early in March 1962. This ship shaft saga had its beginnings when the SS York, a freighter operated by Transwestern Associates, broke down in Hong Kong. Pictures show the Tiger Connie parked on the Hong Kong ramp adjacent to the bay with the shaft just coming out of the plane; the platform which had to be built to get the shaft out of the plane; and the shaft in the cabin after its cross-continental and cross-Pacific run to Hong Kong.

In May 1962, the Flying Tigers CL-44 swing-tail airfreighter was presented for public showing at Newark, San Francisco, and Burbank. It was estimated that upwards of 1,500 shippers and 4,000 visitors visited the aircraft at the receptions in each city. Bebe Smith, left, and Gloria Wall, right, Tiger Girls, joined the event, adding spice to the receptions, photographed with the plane, executives and guests. The Watson Bros. Photography Inc.

The largest single piece of airfreight ever flown: a 35,202-pound turbine rotor for the Oxnard, California generating plant of the Southern California Edison Co. is being unloaded from a Flying Tiger CL-44 N448T at Burbank after a non-stop flight from Newark in June 1962. The huge piece, with skidding, was 39 feet long and six feet high.

Super H N6916C, fleet number 806, at San Francisco. Delivered in April 1957, the aircraft flew for the Flying Tiger Line until 1966.
Mel Lawrence via Jon Proctor Collection

Tiger Charter Sets Record at Los Angeles. A Flying Tiger CL-44 charter flight departed Los Angeles on July 2, 1962 for Amsterdam with 165 Los Angeles County dentists and their families bound for the International Dental Convention held in Cologne, Germany on July 6. The group, headed by Doctor U. William Riedel, President of the Los Angeles County Dental Association, arrived in Amsterdam, and then departed for Cologne. Following the week-long convention, the group toured Germany, Italy, Switzerland, and France, returning to Los Angeles on July 31.

Phil Glickman

Tiger Stewardess And 'Passenger'. In July 1962, Flying Tigers landed two baby African elephants in San Francisco for the San Francisco Zoo, originating in Tanganyika (today Tanzania) and flying via Germany. Carey Baldwin, zoo director (right), told Flying Tiger Stewardess Sandy Scatini to be careful about feeding. Here Sandy takes plenty of precaution, while Baldwin watches warily as she offers a tid-bit.
Air News Photos

Happy Landings. In July 1962, movie star Charles "Buddy" Rogers arrived at Flying Tigers' Burbank terminal in his new Sunbeam Alpine sports car, a silver anniversary wedding gift from his famous wife, Mary Pickford, preparatory to starting a world travel and golf tour to be featured in his new colour television series, "Buddy Rogers Adventurous Hobby". The tour took him around the world to famous golf courses, with Flying Tiger associated in the film as his transportation partner. The 6 Watson Bros. Photography Inc.

Flying Boat. The first Flying Scott Custom boat to come off the production line is shown being loaded at Burbank in July 1962 for air shipment to a waiting customer, Island Sports Stores in Babylon, New York. Jack Oxley, standing, right, leading outboard racing driver and member of the Scott Racing Team, supervises the loading of the boat onto CL-44 swing-tail N451T. With him is Jack Hochadel, left, vice president of the boat building facility.   The 6 Watson Bros. Photography Inc.

The picture, taken at the Ojai Valley Inn during the 26 to 28 July 1962 Flying Tigers and CNAC joint reunion, appeared in the Tiger Rag magazine with the following caption: "Milk grows sturdy bodies, as witness Rossi tapping the supply, which seems to have completely astounded Prescott. Kathy is obviously pleased." From left to right are Rossi, Prescott and actress Katherine Marlowe.

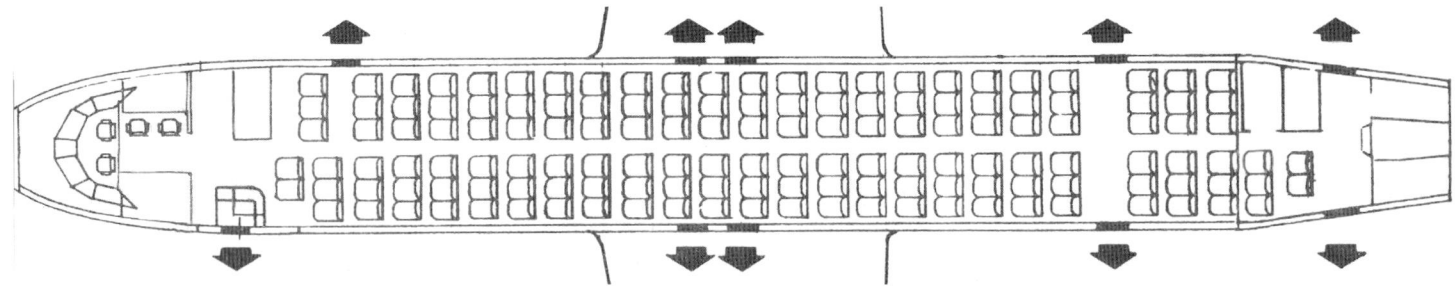

Lessons learned before nose tethers and tail stands. A disembarking passenger inspects the tail of Flying Tiger Line CL-44 N455T at Idlewild on August 1, 1962 which "teeter-tottered" rearwards like a seesaw after about half of the 167 passengers had disembarked at the conclusion of a flight from Paris, leaving an excess of weight in the tail, which settled on the ground "with a gentle thud."

United Press International

Cold Bay, in the Alaska Peninsula, was used by the Flying Tiger Line as a key refuelling location on the Great Circle transpacific route from the United States to the Orient on its many military, cargo and charter flights. Flying Tigers built permanent facilities at Cold Bay including accomodation for crew members and base personnel, and facilities for flight operations and maintenance. In between flights, crew members take a break or enjoy a snooker to pass away the time. Note the PROPERTY OF F.T.L. label on the pool.

Flying Tiger 923 ditching. On September 28, 1962, Super H Constellation N6923C was successfully ditched in the North Atlantic about 500 miles west of Shannon, Ireland, after losing three engines on a flight to Frankfurt, Germany. 45 out of 68 passengers and three out of eight crew survived, a miraclous outcome given the location and conditions. Aviation Photo News via J. Ryan

courtesy of Eric Lindner

Survivors of the Flying Tiger L-1049H N6923C which ditched in mid-Atlantic on September 28, 1962 at the rail of rescue ship Celerina as it neared Antwerp. From left are Master Sergeant Peter A. Foley of South Bend; Captain Juan A. Figueroa-Longo of Santurce, Puerto Rico; his wife, Carmen; flight attendant Carol Ann Gould, holding paper, of Lyndhurst NJ; Captain John D. Murray of Oyster Bay, New York, with bandage over forehead injury; and an unidentified woman.

APWirephoto via radio from London, Houston Post Library

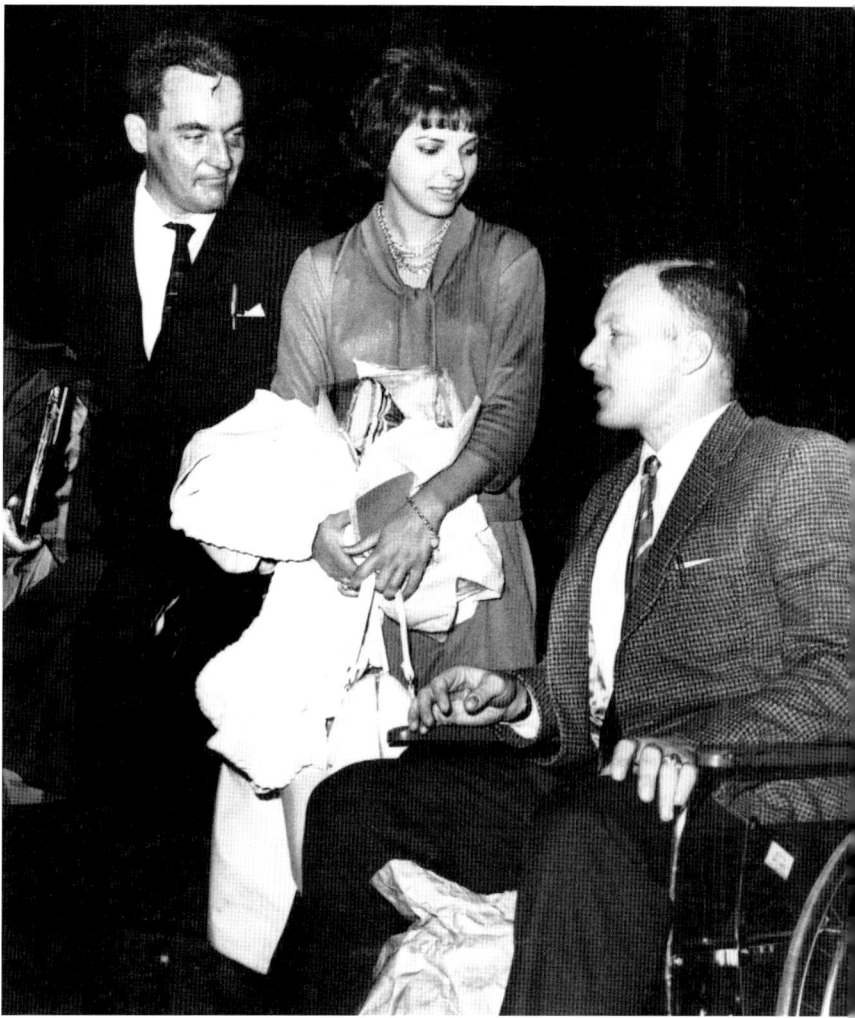

Sam Nicholson (in wheelchair), navigator of the Flying Tiger plane which ditched in the North Atlantic, arrives at New York Idlewild from Brussels on September 30, 1962 with Captain John Murray (left) and Flight Attendant Carol Ann Gould, who were among the 48 survivors of the accident. Nicholson, who was responsible for saving many lives while in the water, suffered burns, while Murray's face was severely bruised. Captain Murray was the last survivor pulled into the raft. Gould, Murray and Nicholson were flown back to the United States on a Sabena Boeing 707-329.

In the early sixties, CL-44s were the backbone of the airline's transpacific charter operations for the Military Air Transport Service (MATS). This unusual scene shows three CL-44s at Kadena Air Base in late 1962, a major US military facility on Okinawa Island, Japan. Military cargo is being unloaded from the two in the foreground while a third in the background is being serviced for a return flight to the United States.

James McLachlan

Michiganders Take Flyer in Florida. A group of 95 people from the Dearborn and Detroit area of Michigan on arrival at Daytona Beach in Florida in May 1963, for a look at the Mackie development at nearby Deltona. They were flown from Detroit in three and a half hours aboard Super Connie N6917C.

When the Pratt & Whitney TF33-P-7 turbofan was approved for both military and civilian flight by the US Air Force and the Federal Aviation Agency, the first production example, weighing 5,832 pounds, was flown aboard a Flying Tiger Super H Constellation from Hartford, Connecticut, to Chula Vista, California, where Rohr Aircraft completed assembly. Designated JT3D on civilian aircraft such as the Boeing 707, the TF33-P-7 originally powered the C-141 Starlifter, fabricated by the Lockheed-Georgia Company in Marietta. Though Tigers placed a $64 million order for eight Lockheed Super Starlifters, or L-300B, on May 12, 1964, with deliveries scheduled for 1967, the civilian C-141 project was later cancelled. Left to right in the picture are cargo loaders Joe Garrett, Francis Bourque and Fernand Ferland.

Flying Tiger stewardesses became their own photographers to snap some of the track stars aboard the flight on June 20, 1963. Left to right on the photography line are Mimi Burns, Mary Van Ouwerkerk and Barbara Wall with their "subjects," left to right, Ralph Boston, champion broad jumper; Parry O'Brien, king of shot putters; and C. K. Yang, decathlon titleholder. The Striders team went on to win.

Phil Hickman

In July 1963, President John Fitzgerald Kennedy greeted Anne-Marie and Robert Prescott on the White House lawn at a reception for the General Claire Lee Chennault Foundation, bestowing presidential endoresement. Prescott was a member of the honorary advisory committee of the foundation, which was formed to provide relief for refugees from mainland (communist) China in memory of General Chennault, fabled wartime leader of the AVG Flying Tigers.

The Belfast Tradesmen's Social Club's Tiger charter flight CW13 of July 7, 1963 from Belfast, to Buffalo, New York, onboard Super H N6916C under the command of Captain Hedden. The group returned home to Ireland on July 30 by the same means.

United Press International

Korean Orphans Fly to U.S. Homes by Tiger Charter. Flying Tiger CL-44 prop-jet, N451T under the command of Captain Stuart J. "Stu" McMahon, departing Los Angeles for Korea on a charter flight to bring orphans to US homes. The flight took place on November 23, 1963, the day after the assassination of President Kennedy. Previously, children were simply flown to the United States, after couples had agreed to adopt them. Under a new law, parents had to see the children before adoption, so the parents flew to Korea to get them. This was the first flight under the new law. Outbound flight crew, stewardesses, left to right, Elizabeth Lambert, Joy Yates, Carolyn Lee, Sally Zajac and Dorothy Martinson, left to right on steps, Captain Stuart J. "Stu" McMahon, Navigator Jack Wanzer, Flight Engineer Hank Germain, and Captain Robert "Skee" Zalusky.   William Eccles Airport Photography

On November 30, 1963, 81 Korean orphans, ranging in age from two weeks to 14 years, flew to new homes in the United States in the arms of 58 couples, most living in Southern California but others from as far afield as Minnesota, Michigan, Indiana and other midwestern states. When it left Seoul, 22 hours earlier, the aircraft had 197 souls on board but one couple and child were left behind in Anchorage, Alaska, where the plane made a customs stop, because of illness of the child, with 194 completing the trip on that date. William Eccles Airport Photography

Korean Orphans, New Parents Fly to U.S by Tiger Charter. The CL-44 landed at Los Angeles International at 9:22 p.m. on November 30, 1963, with 194 persons aboard, believed to be the largest number of persons ever carried in a commercial airliner at the time.

William Eccles Airport Photography

Captain Jim Bledsoe, who piloted the CL-44 plane from Korea with children and parents, says goodbye to two of his charges after arrival at Los Angeles. William Eccles Airport Photography

Missionaries. First of four planeloads of members of the New Zealand Missionary Society of the Mormon Church, en route from Salt Lake City to Honolulu in January 1964, are shown in San Francisco during a stop in what was one of the largest charter operations ever performed by the Flying Tiger Line. Second from the left is Captain George A. Bock. More than 400 members of the society flew to the islands to participate in the dedication of a new Polynesian cultural centre established by the society. In the background is Super H N45516, fleet number 818, leased from KLM from July 1963, originally delivered to KLM on April 14, 1958 as PH-LKL Desiderius Erasmus.

Ralph Demeree - Richard Osborn - Air News Photos

Flying Tigresses. Judith Cotton, 1960 Olympic Games synchronised swimmer receives her wings as one of the first 24 girls to graduate formally as a Flying Tigress in February 1964. Doing the honours on the diving board of the Hilton Inn at San Francisco International Airport is Vye Kisner, SFO flight attendant instructor. Looking on, lower right: Ellen Wiedmann, who was elected most popular by classmates, and Carole Gille, who graduated with the highest grades.

February 1964, deadheading from Tokyo to San Francisco, from the left, Flight Attendants Juanita Hennesey, Lee (?), Marliese Berger and Marjorie Evans, having borrowed the caps of the pilots, are having fun and "riding" a Honda across the Pacific Ocean.

How to wear a lifejacket correctly - brought to you by Marliese (left) and Juanita, both in a state of hilarity.

Marjorie Evans is lifting Juanita to rest in the overhead in the event that all seats are filled with passengers. A perfect place to be!

Photos Juanita Hennessey

Flight Attendant Cecile "CeCe" McCollins Jonsen serving refreshments aboard a CL-44 charter flight in May 1964.
Edwin C. Lombardo, Detroit News

When the Detroit Daily News decided to reward its hard working newpaper delivery boys with a trip to New York to see the World's Fair which ran from April 22 to October 18, 1964, it chose a Flying Tiger charter flight for the trip. Here are the boys, 116-strong, led by L. J. Hamilton of the News, as they got ready to return home after a two-day tour of the fair and the sights of Manhattan.

A new intra-airport service was launched in May 1964 by the Flying Tiger Line at four major terminals, Los Angeles, San Francisco, Chicago and New York, with the introduction of a fleet of interline freight vans to operate between airline and broker offices, picking up or delivering freight brought in by FTL for further movement on other carriers. The trucks, one of which is pictured here at Burbank with Al Cormier, FTL building and facility supervisor, carried 4,200 pounds of freight. Phil Glickman

Flying Tiger AVG Reunion in Taipei July 1-4, 1964. At the invitation of Generalissimo and Madame Kai-Shek, the AVG Tigers gang flew on CL-44 N455T from Los Angeles to Taipei, with stops in San Francisco, Cold Bay and Tokyo. Above photo is somewhere over the Pacific. Slumped way down is Bob Rengo; back a bit is Robert Prescott and the Rodewalds; on left, still in action, is R. T. Smith with cigarette at attention; next to him, Jim Bennett; Don McBride, left foreground. The six house mothers, dressed as flight attendants, on the long flight to Taipei were, from bottom up, Marie Flesher, Ida Lono, Judy Hatch, Ada Gardner, Colleen Carey and Laura Direnzo.

In Taipei on June 30, the AVG Tigers were welcomed with banners, speeches, the whole bit!

Captain Jack F. Morris (above at the door) and Captain Orval A. Prevost jumping down the emergency slide of a CL-44 plane during an evacuation drill.
CL-44.com Collection

Scouts off to Jamboree Via Tigers. Eight planeloads of more than 1,124 energetic, bustling youths flew across the United States in July 1964 in what was one of the largest charter operations ever flown by the Flying Tiger Line: Boy Scouts headed for the sixth national Jamboree at Valley Forge, Pennsylvania. Tiger CL-44s and Super H Constellations carried the boys from Los Angeles, Stockton and Fresno in California, and Salt Lake City and Provo in Utah, on a two-week tour of historic spots of the east, from Boston to Washington. Ralph Samuels Valley Photo

Flying Tiger's swing-tail CL-44 set another all-time record in July 1964 when it exceeded its own record for carrying the largest piece of commercial airfreight ever lifted, a ship shaft weighing 46,262 pounds and destined from the Standard Steel Company of Lewiston, Pennsylvania to the Kobe shipyards. It was flown from Newark to Osaka, exceeding by more than 10,000 pounds the previous record shipment, a 35,202 pound turbine generator flown from Newark to Los Angeles. Significantly, the CL-44 was the only commercial aircraft at the time that could have flown either shipment. The ship shaft was originally tendered to Pan American World Airways, who were forced to turn it down because of inability to handle it. While it required nearly six hours to prepare the aircraft and shaft for loading, the actual loading process took only 45 minutes. The aircraft flew the long journey in two segments, a 12-hour leg from Newark to Anchorage and another 12 hours to Japan.

Tiger in Florida. Flying Tiger Connie N6918C receives service from Butler Aviation at West Palm Beach, Florida, March 1965. The airline carried heavy traffic with winter vacation groups from New York to Florida and the Bahamas.   Michael Roth

Tigers Begin 707 Training. Initial training classes for maintenance and flight crews on the new Boeing 707-320C freighters started in Seattle in March 1965. Vice President James McLachlan (right, in the Boeing 707-320C cockpit simulator) and Superintendent of Engineering Chuck Sleeves (left) headed the first training delegation to the Boeing plant. Each training class took six weeks and upon completion of one group, another was assigned to the Boeing programme.

Ground-breaking ceremonies at Los Angeles International Airport for Flying Tigers' new $4,000,000 general office and maintenance base brought out a large group of construction, airport, engineering and airline executives to turn the first earth on the 25-acre plot which the Tiger base would occupy. Completion was scheduled for the end of 1965. Pictured here is the group on hand for the ground breaking, headed by six executives in the centre foreground. The ceremony had a fun-filled moment when Robert Prescott, sledge hammer in hand, drove the first stake into the ground for a sign marking the Tiger site. Enjoying Prescott's hammer work, which proved to be both safe and accurate, were, left to right, President Bob Haynie of the contracting firm of Haas and Haynie; Ray O. Kusche, president of Quinton Engineers, architects; and Francis Fox, general manager of Los Angeles International Airport.

The 20th anniversary of the Flying Tiger Line was celebrated on June 23, 1965 at the Hollywood Palladium on Sunset Boulevard with 500 business, civic and airline industry leaders. A surprise gift from Tiger employees to Robert Prescott was a China doll, Miki Irish, delivered by Dick Rossi and Cliff Groh (a 20th anniversary present is traditionally china.)

Delmar Watson

The 20th anniversary of the Flying Tiger Line was a perfect occasion for Robert Prescott to be photographed with Tiger Girls.
Delmar Watson

Do you know a Willie? Not the girls, the thing with the furry body and big eyes. Willies, the newest product of the Wham-O-Company, whose hula-hoop set the country afire, reached stores and children across the country, many of them via Flying Tiger Line Wham-O, to illustrate the potential of the Willie, produced a model 60 feet long, and naturally there was only one cargo handler who could move it. Girls were the only answer and here they are, ready to load the king-size Willie on a Tiger CL-44 freighter at Los Angeles in July 1965.

Delmar Watson

Ordered on January 18, 1965, Flying Tigers' first Boeing 707-349C jet freighter, registered N322F, nears completion on the flight line at Renton in August 1965, making its first flight the following month, on September 11, 1965.

In September 1965, a Mitsubishi MU-2B registered JA8629 was exported to the U.S. with a Flying Tiger CL-44. The MU-2 is a Japanese high-wing, twin-engine turboprop aircraft with a pressurized cabin manufactured by Mitsubishi Heavy Industries. It made its maiden flight in September 1963 and is one of postwar Japan's most successful aircraft, with 704 manufactured in Japan at Nagoya Airport and San Angelo, Texas. The "B" model or MU-2B was the first aircraft sold to the public and boasted a top speed of 300 mph at 20,000 feet. This was an impressive feat for 1965. The Astazu engines were replaced with Garrett TPE 331-25AA or -25AB engines and the aeroplane was well stocked with U.S. manufactured electronics, interiors and other components resulting in over 70% of the aircraft being manufactured in the U.S. This model also featured 65 gallon tip tanks which provided a range of 1,150 miles with 45 minute reserve. Stall speed "clean" was 98 mph which was reduced to 74 mph with the full 40° of flaps deployed. JA8629 was the 6th MU-2B built and made its first flight on July 29, 1965.   Photos Delmar Watson

N322F, Flying Tigers' first Boeing 707-349C jet freighter, on the flight line at Renton in August 1965.

Thrilling air-to-air view of N322F in tight formation during a test flight and photo shot over the West Coast.

Boeing 707-320C Burbank Debut. Flying Tigers' first Boeing 707-349C N322F taxis up to the Tiger ramp at the airline's main base at the Lockheed Air Terminal in Burbank, September 27, 1965. The crew on the first flight was Harley Beard, chief of Boeing pilot training; Jack Martin, Flying Tiger Line system chief pilot and flight captain; Flight Engineer Gene Olson of Tiger; and Don Boyd, Boeing chief of flight engineering training.

Several hundred visitors, led by Robert Prescott, went through the big aircraft. Captain Jack Martin flew it into Burbank and then returned it to San Francisco, where it continued in crew training. The aircraft started service on the Pacific in the MATS contract operation on October 22. Delivered a few weeks before, the first Flying Tigers Learjet 23 N242F joined the ceremony by neatly fitting aft of the Boeing wing section. Standing next to the Learjet, left to right, E. A. Pinke, Flying Tiger Line vice-president operations; Lieutenant General L. C. Craigie of FTL's board of directors, who also was the first military pilot ever to fly a jet; M. B. McKinney, vice president of Union Bank; Fred L. Austin of TWA; and Robert Prescott.

Robert Prescott takes two guests on a tour of the cockpit of the first Boeing 707-349C N322F on September 27, 1965 in Burbank: Carole Phillips, Miss Flying Tiger Credit Union, and Ulisse Mazzolini, noted Italian attorney and business leader.

Delmar Watson

Bob and his 11-year son Peter Evans Prescott in Burbank in the cockpit of Flying Tigers Learjet 23 N242F on September 27, 1965. Peter was the only son of Bob and Helen Ruth Prescott. He died on November 14, 1965 in the accident of Learjet sistership N243F following takeoff from Palm Springs to Burbank. Five other persons aboard also were lost. The group had been visiting in Palm Springs and attended the departure of Flying Tiger's Boeing 707-349C N322F on its record round-the-world, pole-to-pole flight for the Rockwell-Standard Corporation.

Pole Cat flight aviation epic sets eight new world records. The Pole Cat, prior to its departure from Burbank Lockheed Air Terminal on November 14, 1965, received a final check before its 26,000 mile polar flight. She was to fly over the North and South Poles in the record-breaking time of 62 hours, 27 minutes from take-off to touchdown in Honolulu, accruing a flight time of 51 hours, 27 minutes over 26,500 miles, the first time that humans had ever flown around the world via both poles. Garry Watson Photography

A new type of auxiliary fuel cells were put aboard to provide extra long-range capability. Each carrying 2,000 gallons of fuel, they were rubber/nylon, collapsible, and incorporated unique tie-down and surge-arresting mechanisms. They were installed on November 11 in the Pole Cat's main cabin, just aft of the cockpit and forward of the passenger compartment. It was the first time these cells were used on a public transport aircraft.

Air Logistics Corporation

Robert Prescott with maintenance crew prior to departure from Burbank on November 14, 1965. From left to right, Fred Stunkel, Charley Pryor, Isodore Holtz, John Munoz, Bob McNally, Bob Prescott, Al Cormier and Dave Phillips. Anderson Photography

After a ferry flight from Burbank, the Pole Cat arrived in Palm Springs on November 14 in pouring rain. Two truckloads of personnel and equipment were positioned to Palm Springs, including an air starter and electrical power unit from San Francisco, engine stands and other ground equipment, so that everything would be shipshape in the desert town, from which the Pole Cat was to depart as part of the International Aeroclassic event staged there. After a few hours in Palm Springs, the Pole Cat took off again, still in the rain, and headed for Honolulu for the official start of her flight around the world.

After London and Lisbon, the Pole Cat arrived in Buenos Aires on November 16, 1965, for a two hour turnaround before its flight to the South Pole and on to Christchurch, New Zealand, and finally back to Honolulu. The plane, loaded with slightly more than 185,000 pounds of fuel, used the entire length of the runway at Buenos Aires before becoming airborne.

Termination of the round-the-world flight. Sunshine greeted the Pole Cat when it landed at Honolulu at the conclusion of its round-the-world, pole-to-pole flight. Crew members in Honolulu, from left to right, Dino G. Valazza, flight engineer, TWA; John Larsen, navigator, Weems Corporation; Captain Fred L. Austin, co-commander, TWA; Loren E. DeGroot, navigator, Lear Siegler; Captain Robert N. Buck, TWA; Captain James R. Gannett, Boeing Aircraft Company; Captain Jack Martin, pilot in command, FTL; Eugene Olson, flight engineer, FTL; James M. Jones, flight engineer, TWA; Captain Harrison Finch, co-commander, TWA; and E. A. Hickman, navigator, FTL.

Rothschild Photo

The Pole Cat was refueled at Honolulu and headed into Burbank in the rain, just as they left! Captain Jack Martin is greeted at the Lockheed Air Terminal by two Tiger Girls. Delmar Watson

L-1049H Super Constellation N6914C in Chicago. The aircraft was lost on December 15, 1965 when it crashed on the southwest face of California Peak, 22 nautical miles northeast of Alamosa, Colorado. The crew consisted of Captain Everett D. 'Pete' Reed, First Officer Thomas Duane Hunt and Second Officer Brian M. Ferris. The crew was performing a scheduled domestic cargo service from Los Angeles to Chicago. While cruising at the assigned altitude of 13,000 by night, in cloud and snow, the crew apparently became disoriented and failed to turn to airways V-210 outbound heading to Alamosa VORTAC as filed, for an undetermined reason.   Jan Boon Collection

Aviation history's first whale lift. On December 24, 1965, Flying Tigers airlifted Shamu the killer whale from Seattle-Tacoma to San Diego aboard CL-44 N455T. Upon arrival in San Diego, cargo handlers unloaded Shamu by stretching a cable from the fork lift to the Shamu's sheepskin-lined cradle in the cargo hold of the CL-44. The lift pulled the heavy cradle, weighing approximately 4,000 pounds including Shamu, to the cargo door and on to another lift, and finally onto a flatbed truck for onward transportation to Sea World. The team of experts who observed Shamu's behaviour during her more than three hours out of water pampered her with generous offerings of salmon and soothed her with a continual ice water sponge bath.